SCHOLARLY EDITION

CHOOSING FOR TWO

An Examination of Abortion Decision Making
and Its Implications for Crisis Counseling

David Ross, PsyD, MDiv

MW MEDIA
PORTLAND

Published in the United States by MW Media, LLC, Portland, Oregon

ISBN: 978-0-9907806-4-9 (pbk.)

Table of Contents

Dedication

This work is dedicated to all the people the world will not get a chance to meet because their lives were brought to a premature end by abortion. If this work saves just one life from the horror of abortion then I will know that my effort was not in vain.

Acknowledgments

I am deeply indebted to my professors who have supported this project and shared their unique talents to guide this challenging process. Dr. Mark Hanna contributed valuable recommendations based on his experience in the field and provided support with editing this project. Dr. Norman Geisler's knowledge and wisdom provided the guidance necessary for assisting me in narrowing my focus. Dr. D. Scott Henderson assisted in examining the bioethical issues involved and provided editing suggestions. Dr. Scott Matscherz generously gave of his time to assist with editing, while also providing counsel, guidance, and encouragement.

My parents have also played an integral role in this process. Thank you to the Rosses for their financial support; the Kitts for opportunities to think through the topics, for intriguing discussion, and for editing support; and the Lazatins for their material support. Lei and I thank you all for the love you have showered us with, especially over the last few years. I would also like to thank the Women's Resource Medical Centers of Southern Nevada for their passion of saving lives, and for providing me with the opportunity to serve those who find themselves in a crisis pregnancy situation.

Lastly, I would like to thank my wife, Lei, for her love, support, and sacrifice which has made this project possible. God blessed me with Lei, my perfect complement serving as my steadfast colleague and friend who acts as a sounding board, an editor, and a wise counsel to direct the development of the flowchart concepts contained in this work.

Foreward by Norman L. Geisler, PhD

Abortion is the number one ethical problem in the United States, if not in the world. Evangelicals have been slow to recognize the reality and severity of the problem. The logic against abortion is painfully clear: 1) It is morally wrong to intentionally take the life of an innocent human being, as virtually all agree. 2) Abortion of unborn babies intentionally kills innocent human beings, a scientific fact established beyond all reasonable doubt. 3) Therefore, abortion is morally wrong.

The statistics on abortion are dreadful. In the US alone we have killed over 55 million unborn human beings by abortion since 1973. At most, Hitler killed only 12 million people. In the US abortions occur at the rate of about 3000 a day. That is several abortions every minute! No other fatal ethical issue even comes close to these statistics. Cancer takes only 585,000 lives annually, whereas abortion takes about 1.5 million!

My first encounter with abortion came when I was protesting at the largest abortion clinic in Dallas, Texas many years ago. Someone had brought a baby to the protest. While it was my turn to hold the baby in my arms, a young girl passed by to enter the clinic for the deadly procedure. Her parents and boyfriend were with her. As they entered the clinic door, the pregnant girl paused at the front. Then she turned and looked directly at me and the baby in my arms. After a brief moment, she turned and walked directly into the clinic to snuff out the life of the little one in her womb. I looked down at the live baby in my arms. It was a life-transforming experience! Two generations have passed and recently my four-year old granddaughter Rachel showed me a picture of the sign she made for the abortion mill she helps protest with her mother and two siblings. It read: "Your baby needs you!" I just cannot imagine any pregnant girl walking past her sweet little face and heart-wrenching sign and killing her baby.

One day my curiosity was piqued at our clinic when I wondered who owned the building they were renting out to kill unborn babies. I wish I hadn't asked. Unbelievably, it turned out to be two Roman Catholic businessmen and an evangelical Christian! I thought I would like to speak to the evangelical. When we met for breakfast, I asked if he knew what was transpiring in his building. He did, but amazingly passed the responsibility on to his wife with whom he inquired before he entered the contract to rent the building to abortionists. She rationalized to him, "Well I would like to think there was a place our daughter could go, if she got into trouble!" When I pointed out that he was profiting from renting a building in which they were regularly killing little unborn human beings, he justified his actions, saying, "If I dropped out of the contract, I would lose thousands of dollars." Dollars over lives! I could not believe my ears. But this is what happens in the US several thousand times daily.

Over the years since then, I have written several books, penned dozens of articles, and given hundreds of lectures on abortion, but have not encountered a more comprehensive, complete, and helpful book than this one. It not only covers the ethics, extent, and implications of abortion, but it provides practical help in counseling those who have contemplated or completed an abortion. Few authors have the academic background, ethical training, and counseling experience to produce a book like this, as Dr. David Ross has done. This book is not merely a complete academic text; it is a life-saving volume. Everything one needs to know about the nature, results, and prevention of abortion is found within these pages. If you get this volume, you will not need another book on the topic.

—Norman L. Geisler, PhD
Professor and author of over 90 books

Chapter One
The Human Impact Of Abortion

Introduction

This book examines the controversial topic of abortion in order to enhance the effectiveness of counselors in persuading pregnant women to carry their children to term. Crucial to fulfilling this purpose is the clarification of the mechanisms involved in choosing to have an abortion and the factors that influence women to make this tragic choice. Those who favor abortion as an elective option see it as a right. They cannot fathom how people can be so adamantly opposed to abortion when from their perspective it is a decision for a woman to make for herself. Those opposed to abortion likewise cannot understand how anyone could ever support abortion as it ends the life of a human being, an unborn child. This controversy has raged for over forty years now, and it does not appear much progress has been made in bridging the gap between the two sides in the debate. It is evident that the two sides are irreconcilably at odds with one another. This author believes this to be the case and will indicate why later, but for now it is sufficient to state that the reason this issue still remains important is that it deals ultimately with the value of human beings.

Only human beings have been created in the image of God, and thus there should be great concern for all individuals. Whether young, old, healthy, or ill, all people are bearers of God's image and deserve to be cared for, protected, and loved as is fit for such a creation. Abortion is not a victimless crime. In fact it is not considered a crime at all in the United States – with some qualifications. But despite the current legal status of abortion, every single person is victimized by abortion in some way.

Clearly the child being aborted is injured when his life is taken. The mother of the child is often haunted by the long term impact in the realms of her psychological, physical, and spiritual functioning. Fathers of aborted children are robbed of the opportunities to be the men that God intends them to be. And certainly human beings are injured when it is arbitrarily decided which human beings have sufficient worth to be protected and which human beings are insufficiently valuable so that their lives can be terminated in the womb.

All people can be hurt by abortion. Still the debate continues, and this author believes the debate will continue regardless of what happens in the courts of this country or around the world. Although it may not be possible to save everyone from the pain associated with abortion, it is possible to save some people. In fact, I believe that by better understanding how decisions are made by women who choose to abort their children, interventions can be developed which offer the compassion, care, and love to those women who likewise face a crisis pregnancy. This book attempts to do just that – to integrate what is known about abortion in general with what the research on decision-making in general and regarding abortion have revealed so that ultimately lives can be saved; not only the lives of the children but also, in some cases, the lives of the women with unintended pregnancies.

To accomplish this, a brief review of human development will be offered. This will establish the biological underpinnings for considering the unborn as human beings. A history of abortion as it has been viewed by society and the church will then follow. As part of this history, the legal status of abortion in the United States will be discussed along with the socio-cultural developments that have occurred which have led to the current intractable debate that we find ourselves in as a nation at the present time.

A review of the abortion debate will be conducted as this book examines the various main arguments espoused by both sides. This will lead into a consideration of world views and why this author believes the abortion debate is not one that is readily amenable to resolution at a societal level. However, this should not rule out the impact that can be made on an individual level, and thus the research regarding decision making will be surveyed in brief. After reviewing the research on general decision-making, the specific factors that seem to be most relevant to the abortion decision for women will be examined.

Lastly, the implications for offering counsel to people facing unintended pregnancies will be discussed. Suggestions for crisis pregnancy counselors and others involved in counseling people faced with the decision to abort their child will culminate in a flowchart which will synthesize the material in this book so that it is in a readily available and accessible format for counselors.

Human Development – How A Person Begins Their First Nine Months Of Life

The advances in science have done a tremendous service in helping to illuminate the process in which a human being moves from a single celled organism to the point of the brain's complete maturity outside the womb, which occurs around the age of twenty-five. It is now possible to actually obtain images from the time of conception all the way to the time that a child is delivered. In light of these advances, it is now possible to visually observe what transpires from the very moment that a new human being is created as a sperm fertilizes an egg.

Prior to Conception

As the developmental process is examined, it is interesting to note that the process that leads to the formation of a new human organism begins at the very earliest stages of development. This means that the mature sperm cells and mature egg that ultimately unite to form a new being do not just come into existence prior to conception. Rather, the structures and processes involved in the production of these cells begins when a male or female is only a few months of age. Although men continue to generate sperm cells throughout their adult lives, the process of gametogenesis, the making of gametes or sex cells, begins when men are in the embryonic state.[1] For women the same is true even though women differ in that they are born with all the eggs they will ever possess.

Gametes, known also as sperm and egg cells, are the sex cells found in human beings. In males, the sperm cells are formed in the testicles. While in females the egg cells are formed in the ovaries. Even though men and women are born with the necessary structures, and in the case of women all the egg cells she will possess, the male and female do not begin to produce mature gametes until they reach adolescence and hormonal signals initiate puberty, causing their bodies to begin to produce the mature sex cells capable of reproduction.

Conception

Sperm cells are part of the man's body and the egg cell is part of the woman's body. However, when a sperm cell fertilizes an egg, the result is that the newly formed entity is genetically distinct from either parent. The moment of fertilization is referred to as conception, which involves the fusion of the genetic materials from the individual sperm and egg cells. This process of conception involves a dynamic interaction between the sperm and egg cell in which both cease to be and a new and different cell comes into being. This new cell, which contains its own unique genetic code, is different from either parent and is called a zygote. Although both the male and female parent contributed their genetic material through their respective gametes, the zygote is truly genetically unique as a result of the process in which the twenty-three chromosomes of each of the gametes have fused to form a new cell with forty-six chromosomes.

Even though sperm cells and egg cells are oriented towards joining with the opposite type of gamete, once fertilization occurs the zygote forms a barrier to keep other cells from penetrating its external boundaries. This further indicates that this new cell has been transformed into a different type of entity. The zygote now is no longer a sperm cell, an egg cell, or even a simple combination of both per se, but rather a unique and separate organism since it possesses a unique genetic code and is able to independently direct its own growth and development. Neither sperm nor egg cells possess the capability to grow or direct their own development, and this signifies that indeed something remarkable has occurred through the dynamic fusion that is known as conception. As a result of the fact that the zygote contains all the genetic material that this particular human being will ever possess, "many people define this as the moment life begins."[2]

From a scientific perspective, the zygote is a unique human organism that is distinctly different from either the man or woman from which the sperm and egg were obtained. This can be illustrated with the knowledge that individuals conceived in Petri dishes can be implanted in the wombs of women who have not contributed to their genetics biologically. Thus it is possible to implant a zygote from Asian parents into the womb of a woman of African ethnicity and the child which is born will still be of Asian descent. From a scientific perspective, the womb is merely a biological incubator, offering a safe and proper environment in which the newly created human organism will continue to grow.

This new organism, a zygote, is now able to direct its own growth and development on its way towards full maturity with the genetic code it possesses. The zygote begins to grow by the normal process of internally directed cellular division. In fact, the developmental process is completely internally driven and is not reliant on outside forces to provide direction during the growth process. The only external requirements are support; the provision of food, oxygen, and a safe environment. These external requirements continue to be necessary for all living beings regardless of their level of development in order for them to grow, develop, and continue life. If provided with these essentials, the new human being will grow towards maturity and then continue to progress towards a natural death barring no unforeseen circumstances.

In light of the scientific evidence, it is unmistakable that a zygote is indeed a new human being. From this point forward the new human being will be referred to as a child and given a personal pronoun to reflect accurately the nature of the being under discussion.

First week

The first task for the new child is to travel down the fallopian tube towards the uterus. This process takes five to six days before the child will reach the uterus and be ready to implant in the uterine wall. During this time her cells will continue to divide every twelve to fifteen hours until she reaches a size of approximately one hundred cells. After just under one week of life, the child has reached the uterus where she will stay for the next nine months.

Second week

The major developmental milestone attained during the second week of life is the development of the primate streak. This observable feature is known to be the precursor to the human nervous system and is observable about twelve to seventeen days after conception.

Third week

Only three weeks after coming into the world at the moment of conception, the child's heart begins to beat. Within a few days her heart is beating rhythmically and the blood which circulates in her body is often totally different than the mother's blood. The child has a separate circulatory system from the mother, which is why her blood type can be completely different from the mother's.

By the End of the First Month

After only four weeks of development the child's face and limbs have formed. Her eyes, nose, and mouth have formed even though she is only about one quarter of an inch in length. Additionally her liver, kidneys, and digestive tract have begun to form as her body further forms and differentiates into the various organ systems.

By the End of the Second Month

Around six to eight weeks of development, the child begins to take on the form of a small human being. The child also has developed some reflexes, and her brain waves have been detectable since about forty days after conception. Many of her organs have already begun to function, such as her kidneys and her stomach. Her heart continues to beat while nerve impulses coming from the brain direct the muscles of her body to contract. At this point in the child's development she engages in regular motion which stimulates the growth process.

By the end of the eighth week all the major organs have formed and the child has taken on a distinctly human appearance. By the end of the second month her eyes, fingers, toes, nose, and skeleton have all developed and are identifiable. Her heart continues to beat and circulate her unique and individual blood.

By the end of the second month no further structural elements develop as everything in the child's body has already begun to take form. The child will continue to develop and mature until approximately twenty-five years of age when full growth is achieved.

By the End of the Third Month

By the end of the ninth week the child has fingerprints which are observable on her fingers which were formed by six weeks of development. These are her unique fingerprints which she will bear for the entirety of her life. Also by this time, the child's sexual organs have developed to the point where a boy can be distinguished from a girl with the naked eye.

By the end of the ninth week the child's kidneys are formed and functioning, indicating that she is able to urinate. By the end of the tenth week all of the child's organs are in place and her gallbladder is already secreting digestive juice.

As early as eight or ten weeks after conception the child is able to feel pain, cry, and engage in movement, such as sucking on her thumb. She is able to grasp with her hands, suck her thumb, and swallow at this point in her development. Her vocal cords have also developed by this time. During the third month the child begins to engage in much more movement, and by the end of the third month she would be able to make noise if she were in the presence of air as her vocal cords have developed sufficiently.

By the end of the twelfth week all the organs which were formed at six weeks are now functioning and no further organs are added. From this point forward all that transpires in the development of the child is growth and maturity of the various organ systems.

By the End of the Fourth Month

Around the end of the fourth month the child's eyelids have formed and completely cover her eyes, which will not open until week twenty-six. She already has tiny hairs covering the skin on her face, and she is approximately seven inches in length and weighs around a quarter of a pound.

By the End of the Fifth Month

By the end of the fifth month the child's hearing has developed sufficiently for her to hear sounds outside the mother's body. She is also able to respond to the maternal voice.

Fingernails are now visible on the child's hands at this point in her development and REM sleep is possible having been observed in children during the fifth month of development. Since REM sleep is associated with dreaming, this suggests that she may be dreaming during her sleep as early as five months into her development.

By the end of the fifth month or just over twenty weeks, the child is now at a stage in her development in which living in the womb may not be necessary. A child twenty weeks post conception is currently deemed to be viable as some babies have survived outside of the womb once they have achieved this developmental age.[3] However, the age of viability is expected to continue to move to earlier time periods as medical technology continues to advance. It is conceivable that at some point in the future that the age of viability will coincide with conception itself—that is, in the sense that sufficient nutritional and environmental conditions could be provided outside the womb.

By the End of Pregnancy – Ninth Month

By the end of the eighth month the child has reached a weight of four and one half to six pounds and will typically gain another two pounds prior to being delivered at full term, which is normally thirty-seven to forty-two weeks. Her delivery will occur when contractions are triggered by hormones in the mother's body. These hormones lead to a series of uterine contractions that force the child through the birth canal and out into the world. For the child this is basically a change of location into a new environment.

Vignettes of Women Who Chose to Abort Their Child

After the foregoing brief survey of the normal development of the child in her mother's womb, it is time to examine what occurs when this process is deliberately terminated. Although it is obviously impossible to get a report from the child in the womb, we can try to imagine what it would be like to have the necessities of life such as oxygen removed or to be dismembered limb from limb. Given the horror that this raises in all but the most hardened of people, how could a mother do this to her own child? Let us now consider the experiences of a few women who have chosen to abort their child's life.

Typically it is only women under duress who contemplate terminating their child's life. It is well documented that many women are in fact forced through threat or coercion to terminate the life of their child. Unfortunately, this coercive pressure often comes from those closest to the women, such as parents, boyfriends, or husbands. Dr. Angelo cites an anecdote about one woman's report of her abortion experience.

> *My boyfriend told me if I kept it, it would break us apart. I loved him and I went and destroyed a life which I wanted so much. I was eighteen weeks pregnant, it took me three days for the operation. Men don't understand what you go through and I wish they did. Throughout the three days I had needles all the time and nausea. This was because of love. I always think of other people before my own feelings, but look at where it's gotten me.... I felt empty, like I had no soul in me.... My boyfriend said to me a couple of days afterwards that we might end up being married and we could have a family together. I said I*

couldn't marry someone that made me destroy a baby.[4]

Although this woman chose to abort her child, she did so "because of love" for her boyfriend. Sadly, she discovered that love has little room for ending the life of another person. It is apparent that this woman certainly regretted her choice. Another anecdote that illustrates the deep levels of regret and pain that women experience when they end the lives of their children is the story told by Judy Mamou about her experience with abortion.

It's been a long time since the lights went out and the doctors went home. But the memory of the few hours I spent in an abortion clinic will be with me to my grave.

I remember the fear I felt lying in the cold white room surrounded by men and women in clean white uniforms. I remember the cold metal stirrups I was told to put my feet in and the cold metal instrument that was inserted into my body to open me up. Most of all I remember the suction machine sucking the life of the baby from within me. The sound of the baby being vacuumed out never goes away.

The doctor may act very kindly and assure you that it will all be over in a few minutes. But how can it be, when you later discover or realize that they lied when they told you it wasn't a person inside you?

Where is the doctor now as I lie here in the still of the night hearing the noise of the vacuum, feeling the cold of the metal and seeing in my mind's eye the bits and pieces of my baby being sucked through the tube of the suction machine? Where was the doctor all those years that I woke up screaming, hearing babies crying in the night?

The sound of the suction machine haunts me to this day. I cannot vacuum a floor without thinking of my abortion.

I never look at a child and not wonder; was mine a boy or a girl; blonde or brunette; my baby would be that age if only...

I've been raped, beaten, a victim of incest and many other things in life but the thing that haunts me most is I let people kill a child of mine. I didn't know at the time that it was a life. I was told it was a blob, matter, nothing, like a tumor to be removed. One day it hits you; it was not a blob or a mass of tissue. It was a BABY!

I can never undo what I allowed to happen but with the forgiveness I have from Jesus I can live with it and do my part to help others not to make the same mistake I did.[5]

Having read Judy's experience, this author finds it hard to think that any woman could view it differently after having an abortion. However, there are many women who have abortions and seemingly have little or no regret or subsequent psychological distress. Here is Sharon's story as reported by Anne Runkle. Sharon is a woman in her late twenties who desires a career and is already in a committed relationship.

On a spiritual level, deciding to have an abortion was very difficult. There were times when I felt clear, and at other times when I felt maybe I was doing something wrong. My boyfriend and I are thinking about marriage, but we're really focused on our goals right now. ... We've worked for these goals too hard to lose it right now. Still, I thought maybe God was saying this is the time and I'm choosing the time for you. We have to ask ourselves – is it time?

I loved being pregnant. Even though I was sick as a dog and lethargic, I felt beautiful and different from what I normally feel. I think he saw that. He was very attentive and nurturing, 200 percent more than ever before, even though he's that way already. The whole time we both knew that we were going to have an abortion. It wasn't going to be too far. That's what made it even more beautiful. We knew that in the future we were going to have kids and it would be perfect. We'll have our house and we'll have our careers. He said before the pregnancy, "When you get pregnant, I want the focus to be completely on the pregnancy, not on school and where we're going to get the next dollar." Of course I cried days and nights – it was sad but I think it was more the hormones that threw me off. In the back of my mind I knew that this wasn't the time…

I had a lot of fear when it came down to the abortion itself. My boyfriend mentioned a lot of nervousness and not wanting to come in the room with me. My mom said, "He really should be in there with you because he helped create it and you made this decision together." I told him I really needed to have him with me. I was going to be put under [general anesthesia] and all this incest stuff came up, and it was going to be a male doctor so it was really important to me that my boyfriend be there. He said he was really scared, and I saw that it wasn't just me in this situation. I had to pay attention to him and let him know I understood. He ended up going in with me….

I told my family. My mom was more afraid that I would regret my decision and she wanted my boyfriend and me to talk through it. I said we'd talked through it numerous times and we were clear. She really wanted a grandchild and that really added to my fears. My sister's been trying to get pregnant for years and years. She even offered to take the baby, but that was definitely out of the question because she's not stable emotionally or financially. I didn't want anybody else to bring up our child. Plus, I made a decision a long time ago that I would break the cycle of dysfunction, and I plan to do everything I can to make my children's life as different as I can.

I feel completely peaceful about my decision. Right after the abortion I felt relief – you know, I get my life back! There were so many things put on hold until I could get through the abortion and heal from it. I couldn't get the energy to take care of things. I think God is okay with it. When I had a car accident recently it brought me back to the abortion; it made me think I was being punished. I always wonder whether on a spiritual level it was right or wrong – will I have to face it when I die? It's always there. It probably always will be. I have fears I won't be able to have kids and I think – What if that was my only chance? What if something happened to me or my boyfriend and we couldn't have kids? I think the changes I went through were normal and healthy. The only thing that could have made it easier is if I had some spiritual guide come to me and say, "This is what you really need to do."

It won't happen again. We've decided that we're not going to have intercourse until we want to have a child....We're so strong on not having to have an abortion again that we're willing to put that part of our sex life aside....

Still, I don't look back with regret. I feel good about what we did. I don't even regret getting pregnant; that in itself was a gift. I know now what I'm going to have to go through when I'm pregnant. I was given a taste of it, of what that would be like. I got to see how my boyfriend

would react with me, and he's going to be the best father.
I feel like that was a real gift.[6]

From Sharon's own report it is evident that she was conflicted over the choice to abort her child. Clearly it had an impact on her, and yet Sharon is similar to many of the women who have undergone abortions. For even though she knows she ended the life of her child, she has convinced herself that having done so was the best possible alternative and ultimately a "gift" in her life.

What makes Judy different from Sharon? How did Judy or Sharon reach a point in their thinking that even entertained the option of killing their children? From the above accounts it should be obvious, even when women choose to abort their children, that this is a difficult decision for them. The days of American women believing that their developing child was just a "lump of tissue" are basically gone, and now an increasing number of women in the United States understand that they are choosing to end the life of a human being when they consent to an abortion.

So what leads women to knowingly end the life of a human being nonetheless? This author believes that women choose to abort their children even though they know they are ending a human life because of numerous factors that impact upon their decision making. These factors range from various (1) sociological pressures, such as women feeling that they must choose to abort their child so that they can maintain the feminine role that our culture has espoused over the last four decades; (2) psychological factors, such as the belief that to maintain their life objectives and the life trajectory they imagine for themselves, they must abort their child; and (3) theological factors, such as who ultimately is the giver of life and the determiner of right and wrong. These various factors are all believed to play a significant role in the decision-making process that women go through as they decide what they will do when faced with an unintended pregnancy.

Chapter Two

A History Of Abortion

Abortion In The Ancient World

To understand abortion in the modern context it is necessary to trace how abortion has been viewed throughout history. Examining the historical, social, and legal views of abortion illuminates how abortion has come to be what it is today, a topic that polarizes society and people. In light of the extent to which the view of abortion has been shaped by the Judeo-Christian tradition, the biblical perspective and the church's understanding will also be discussed.

Abortion is a practice that is deeply embedded in many cultures. What is meant by this is that culture is more than just the ideas and values of a society. Culture also encompasses the tangible goods, such as technology, as well as conduct and action. The fact that abortion has been utilized by women for as long as history has been recorded indicates that it has always been a part of human culture. Some have proposed that since people from all walks of life practiced abortion in the ancient world, there was somehow agreement about abortion being acceptable. Anna Runkle goes so far as to say that the Greek and Christian philosophers generally agreed that abortion was acceptable prior to the time at which the first fetal movements were noticeable – known as the time of quickening.[1]

However, Runkle's reasoning that what is practiced is deemed acceptable does not seem consistent with the other historical accounts. Abortion was practiced by people from all walks of life and religious affiliations in the ancient Greco-Roman world, but it was the pagan peoples who utilized abortion with greater frequency.[2] Of course, both Jews and Christians occasionally had abortions, but the actions of a few are not representative of these groups of people as a whole.

Abortion was more common among the wealthy who did not want to share their estates with numerous offspring. However, the poor also had abortions often due to the perception that they would be unable to support large families. But the most frequent reason that people had abortions was to conceal illicit sexual activity.[3] It would appear that the reasons for women choosing to have abortions have changed little over the last few thousand years.

Abortion methods in the ancient world can be categorized into either chemical or mechanical methods. Interestingly, this is still true to this day. As for chemical methods, a variety of substances were believed to induce abortion and were often "introduced directly into the womb via the birth canal."[4] Many of these remedies involved the introduction of toxic douches and suppositories. Other remedies were to be taken by mouth with the belief that they would induce abortion. These oral remedies were often described as potions, implying that there may have been a belief that they had some supernatural efficacy in bringing about the desired result. Despite the various descriptions of such agents, it is believed that many of them were very ineffective as abortifacients.

Mechanical techniques to induce abortion were numerous as well. One technique described was to bind the woman's body tightly around her womb and then strike her in an attempt to expel the fetus. Other techniques were more consistent with our modern day approach in which copper needles and tools were used to open the uterus, dissect the fetus, and then extract the fetus. Other mechanical techniques attempted to remove the fetus in whole, or when that failed to cut up the fetus and extract it in pieces. In the ancient world, women having abortions later in their pregnancy were certainly at significant risk of dying themselves.

Despite the gruesome thought of poisoning, expelling, or dismembering an unborn child, it should be noted that the killing of children was not uncommon in the ancient world. Historical documents have suggested that although abortion was practiced to terminate the lives of unwanted children, it was in fact exposure that was the preferred Greek method of ending the lives of children who were not wanted. Exposure was the act of taking a newly born child and abandoning the child, leaving the infant to die. It was called "exposure," as the child was left exposed to the elements without care. This was an act of infanticide that was generally deemed acceptable as a practice to limit the size of families or more broadly as a means of controlling population growth.

Infanticide was justified in the ancient Roman world as the legal and moral climate was determined by the power of the father who was perceived to have absolute control over his wife and children. Naturally, this dominion of the Roman man extended to the unborn carried by his family members. Thus, a man in ancient Rome could order his wife or children to be killed. This included the father's prerogative to utilize exposure as a means for eliminating newly born children that he determined were unwanted.

Despite the practice of infanticide in the ancient Greco-Roman world, there is only sparse evidence about the legal opinion regarding abortion in ancient Greece. In light of the fact that exposure of newborns was common and went unpunished, it is hardly surprising that abortion was also unpunished.

There is some evidence that the Hippocratic Oath from the fourth to fifth century B.C. contained a prohibition against abortion, and yet there is not strong evidence to demonstrate that physicians actually adhered to this oath. Some who doubt the authenticity of the abortion prohibition in the oath have suggested that Hippocrates himself provided information to people who desired to have an abortion. Regardless, the oath was accepted among Jews and Christians and has become the medical ethics standard regarding abortion to this day. Despite the cultural acceptance of abortion in the Greco-Roman world, the Jews and Christians had the input of the Scripture which governed their conduct and as such, due to Scriptural prohibition, their view toward abortion tended to be different from that of the populace as a whole.

People without the Scriptures were left to understand the world through their best attempts at reasoning and philosophy. Despite medical ethics which likely opposed abortion, philosophers in ancient

Greece tended to endorse abortion in certain circumstances. In Plato's *Republic* he discusses how all pregnancies in women over the age of forty should be aborted.[5] Plato believed that the state's needs were to take precedence over the rights of the unborn, and thus he encouraged abortion in older women who may have children whom they could not care for properly.

In a somewhat like-minded manner, Aristotle also recommended abortion in addition to the practice of exposure. These approaches were discussed by Aristotle as methods which were employed to limit family size. It appears that both Aristotle and Plato supported abortion on utilitarian grounds, believing that the rights of the state superseded those of individuals.[6] Elements of this early philosophical thought still surface today when abortion is justified as necessary to prevent the strain on society as a whole.

There is some evidence that the Stoics opposed abortion due to their support of large families. However, despite their opposition, the Stoics still did not believe that the fetus possessed a life of its own prior to birth, and thus the Stoics ultimately shared Plato and Aristotle's view that the welfare of the family and the state were more important than the rights or the life of the unborn.

It should come as no surprise that murder was commonplace given the seemingly low view of human life that was present in the first century B.C. At this time in history, the unborn child was viewed as part of the maternal viscera. Hence, the unborn was not seen as a separate individual human being. Thus, those performing abortions or recommending abortifacients would only be held responsible for wrongdoing if they harmed the woman herself.

There was also an increase in antisocial conduct during the first century which led some to see moral decay as a significant societal problem that needed to be addressed. Cicero is noted to have spoken out against the moral laxity in his day including abortion which he opposed. Although Cicero's reasons for opposing abortion did not seem to be related to the well-being of the unborn child or the mother, they were more consistent with the Roman belief related to the rights of the father. Cicero was not opposed to abortion on the basis that it killed an unborn child. Rather, he saw abortion as being unfair or unjust to the father.[7] As the Caesars came to power in the first century

B.C. and the following century, abortion remained at an all-time high and the practice was widespread and perhaps even perpetuated by many of the Caesars.

Although a number of people began to speak out against abortion, it did not appear as if their reason for objecting had anything to do with concern for the unborn child. As the attitude of many regarding abortion began to change during the first century A.D., abortion was still widespread. Differing groups of people began to speak out against the practice, some of them even based their objections on moral grounds. As previously mentioned, the Stoics philosophically condemned abortion on the grounds that it went against the value of having a large family. But there are a number of reports of people during this time who began to equate abortion with being unnatural and nearly on par with murder. This certainly was consistent with the Judeo-Christian perspective, but still was not widely adopted by most of the populace. Others who condemned abortion saw the practice as setting a bad example for others. Again, the concern was not for the unborn child, which is understandable in view of the historical context of the Roman law which did not recognize the unborn as a person. In fact, under Roman law a child was valued not for himself but for his usefulness to his father.

Ultimately, it was both pagan and Christian individuals who engaged in efforts to limit the number of abortions that were taking place. Abortion continued to be widely practiced in the Roman Empire despite the efforts of those opposed to abortion. In fact, legislation to limit abortion did not occur until the third century A.D.

To understand the basis of the Christian perspective at the time, it is necessary to look to the Jewish perspective regarding abortion, which had many similarities with the way Roman law viewed the practice. For instance, a woman whose life was threatened by the unborn child during delivery would be seen as the victim of an attack by an aggressor, namely the child. In these circumstances, abortion was the course of action that was expected to be taken. The mother's life was given precedence and valued over the life of the child by both the Roman secular and Jewish codes of law.

However, there is very little evidence suggesting that Jews practiced abortion on a regular basis. The Jews, also known as the people of the book, as their religious, social, and legal lives were shaped by the Old Testament (OT) Scripture, had a culture based on their conviction that God had revealed his will in the Scriptures. In the Jewish orientation towards life, both abortion and infant exposure were unacceptable as they saw themselves as having a religious duty of begetting children. They saw the need to have children to continue their survival as well as recognizing the value of a child's life. Furthermore, the Jews had been given strict guidelines for when the shedding of blood should be allowed.[8]

The rabbinic writings further suggest that in the Hebrew culture, deliberate abortion was not tolerated or accepted. Rather, most of the writings concern miscarriage. Deliberate abortion would be seen as the shedding of blood and diminishing God's divine image amongst his people, which could lead to the Lord's departing from Israel. Thus deliberate abortion did not receive support in the Jewish culture.

Despite the Jewish perspective being based on one set of religious writings, there were still two schools of thought which differed somewhat on the subject of abortion. The Alexandrian school and the Palestinian schools. The Alexandrian school was influenced by Greek philosophical ideas and by the actual pagan practice of abortion. The Palestinian school of thought focused on the concept of ensoulment of the unborn in determining how to view abortion. However, both schools condemned elective abortion.

Philo of Alexandria understood that the formed fetus could be murdered. He did differentiate between the unformed and formed fetus and saw that the loss of an unformed fetus required a fine whereas the interruption or death of the formed fetus would require death of the perpetrator. Philo saw the issue of abortion as being related to the command in Exodus against murder. Thus Philo saw abortion as a moral issue, an issue of right and wrong and what ought and ought not to be done. Philo's distinction between the formed and unformed fetus has philosophical echoes which can be seen in today's discussion of abortion when the concept of viability is introduced. The worth of the unborn is perceived as varying and dependent upon whether the child is in the pre-viable or the post-viable state.

In the Palestinian school of thought, ensoulment of the unborn seemed to occupy more room in the discussion regarding abortion.

It was generally believed that the fetus was formed after forty days and thus the fetus did not receive status as a child until after this time period. Interestingly, the rabbinical writings do not seem as concerned about the death of a person, the unborn child, but rather about the issue of cleanness or uncleanness of the woman as it pertained to miscarriage in most circumstances.

There were therefore two views, the Alexandrian and the Palestinian. According to the Alexandrian view punishment was required for anyone who damaged a fetus and the punishment was dependent upon the stage of development of the fetus. The Palestinian view which was seen as more lenient held that the fetus was not a person and punishment was only required if the mother was harmed by some action of a person. Again, these two views must be viewed in the context of accidental or therapeutic abortion, not in the context of deliberate abortion. Both schools of thought condemned deliberate abortion as bloodshed.

Thus this Jewish perspective was carried over to the earliest Christian believers who were Jewish converts. The early Christian writings, including the New Testament (NT) books, were opposed to the shedding of innocent blood. In the *Didache,* which is believed to have been written in the late first or early second century A.D., it is declared that, "...you shall not murder a child by abortion nor kill that which is born."[9] This is included in a list of prohibitions which are seen as contrary to loving your neighbor as yourself. The *Didache* also discusses the way of death which includes those people who murder children. This can be seen as additional evidence against those who engage in abortion or infanticide.[10]

Thus the *Didache* serves as one of the earlier Christian writings which equates abortion with murder. No distinction is made between the formed or unformed fetus, but rather the fetus at all stages can be said to require protection and proper care if persons are to be consistent with loving their neighbor. Mistreatment of the fetus at any stage is seen as a definite evil, a grave sin which is forbidden and to be avoided.

The early Church Fathers continued the belief that abortion was morally wrong as it took the life of a human being. Clement of Alexandria held to the concept that abortion was killing a human life. In fact, the understanding that those having an abortion were culpable for taking a human life, and were in essence murderers, began to develop in the first century Christian writings. This thinking was maintained by subsequent writers, two of whom were Athenagoras and Tertullian.

Athenagoras, who lived in the second century A.D., described women who induce abortions as murderers who will have to give an account to God. He claims in his writings to represent the commonly accepted Christian opinion.[11] This position is consistent with the teaching in the *Didache* that abortion is a grave sin, which lends further credence to Athenagoras' claim that his writings were indeed representative of Christian thinking in the second century.

Another Church Father who opposed abortion was Tertullian. He also took the position that the fetus was a human being, even though the fetus was still dependent upon the mother. He describes destroying the fetus in the womb as murder. Tertullian was of the belief that procreation produces both soul and body and that conception is the starting point of life.[12]

Even though all Christian writers generally opposed abortion, the influence of pagan thought on the church did exert some influence on it. This influence manifested itself in Christian women who continued to engage in the practice of abortion. Just as is seen today, a person's actions are not always consistent with his or her beliefs. But social engagement often leads to influence, and it is likely that the Christian writers and apologists also impacted Roman thinking about abortion, as can be inferred from the legislative changes that were implemented. Thus it is likely that Christians contributed to the antiabortion statutes that were ultimately put into effect in Rome during the third century.

It should be noted that the Christian writers of the first three centuries, including the NT authors, developed the understanding based in Scripture about abortion. The conclusions that were reached included that the fetus is an unborn child created by God, that abortion is therefore murder, and, thus, the judgment of God will fall on those practicing it.[13] Further, it was suggested that the child should have human status from the time of conception.

Biblical Passages Pertaining To Abortion

Having examined the conclusion reached by the early Jewish and Christian writers, I now turn to a consideration of the Scriptural basis from which such conclusions were drawn. There are two primary concepts contained in the Scripture. First, the concept that it is God who is the creator, giver, and sustainer of life. Second, the concept that the unborn child is considered by God to be a human being from the moment of conception. Thus a sampling of biblical passages will be examined that illustrate both of these concepts as well as a few passages that actually tie the two concepts together. Looking to see what the Scripture says is crucial for Christians as any analysis of reality must begin with the underlying presupposition that all truth is of God who truly is the final arbiter of knowledge for all people and society. "God must have not only the last say – he must have the first" in all matters of ultimate reality and moral reasoning.[14]

God is the Creator and Giver of Life

This is the book of the generations of Adam. When God created man, he made him in the likeness of God. Male and female he created them, and he blessed them and named them Man when they were created. When Adam had lived 130 years, he fathered a son in his own likeness, after his image, and named him Seth. (Gen. 5:1-3, ESV)

In this passage it is God who creates both man and woman. God tells us that crimes against people are serious as people are made in God's image, and thus an attack against a human being is in essence an attack against God. Furthermore, this passage details God's plan for men and women to have children in their "own likeness" to carry on the human race. God, as the creator or beginner of the human race, is the only one who can truly stake claim to the life of any human being.

You shall not murder. (Exo. 20:13)

This is the sixth commandment given by God to Moses on

Mount Sinai. This commandment makes it clear that humans are not authorized to take the lives of other human beings unless in accord with God's laws as elsewhere given. Generally the taking of human life is an activity left to God or to the governing body and is not delegated to individuals. Since God alone is the giver and maintainer of life, God can and has determined that anyone who takes another life without being given the authority to do so by God is a murderer.

God has commanded that a person who murders another person (first-degree murder), shall have his blood shed. Only a first-degree murder was a capital murder which required the perpetrator to be put to death. All other violations of the law had alternate penalties or punishments which were allowed.[15]

> *You shall not give any of your children to offer them to Molech, and so profane the name of your God: I am the Lord. (Lev. 18:21)*

This passage addresses two things. First and foremost, God is prohibiting parents of children from killing their children. Secondly, God is reemphasizing his command that people are to only worship God and no others. This passage again conveys that God is the rightful owner of the lives of children, and as such can dictate how children are to be treated.

> *You shall not take vengeance or bear a grudge against the sons of your own people, but you shall love your neighbor as yourself: I am the Lord. (Lev. 19:18)*

This passage contains the commandment from God that people are to love other people as they love themselves. When recognizing an unborn child as a human being who can be thus considered a neighbor, it becomes an imperative to treat the unborn in the same way and with the same concern that a person would treat themselves. Hence, no rational person would try to harm or kill themselves, and by God's command this means that it is not proper to harm or kill an unborn child.

God will judge those who turn from judging immorality in their society. I myself will set my face against that man and will cut him off from among his people, because he has given one of his children to Molech, to make my sanctuary unclean and to profane my holy name. And if the people of the land do at all close their eyes to that man when he gives one of his children to Molech, and do not put him to death, then I will set my face against that man and against his clan and will cut them off from among their people, him and all who follow him in whoring after Molech. (Lev. 20:3-5)

In this passage God describes how He will judge both those who have their children killed as well as those who sit by and do nothing as others kill their children. In Israel it was a crime punishable by death to sacrifice a child, and thus God is reiterating the seriousness of murdering an innocent child. Unlike Israel, who in the past sought to function in accord with the Scriptures, the United States has abandoned using the Scriptures as the basis for guiding the civil and criminal legal codes. As such, there is no penalty for ending the life of an unborn child when the death results from an elective abortion. Although historically, a person who killed an unborn child was to be put to death, today this is no longer the situation. No longer does the government seek to exact such punishment and thus people are left to follow the example of Jesus who has commanded that people love their enemies and pray for them. Therefore, we are to pray for those who continue to kill their children, praying that they will seek the forgiveness that is available in Christ alone for this sinful act.

But if he struck him down with an iron object, so that he died, he is a murderer. The murderer shall be put to death. (Num. 35:16)

Again in this passage God makes it clear that to kill another human being willfully and without cause makes a person a murderer. The penalty for murder is death. God has the right to dictate the penalty as the life that was taken belonged to Him.

I call heaven and earth to witness against you today, that
I have set before you life and death, blessing and curse.
Therefore choose life, that you and your offspring may
live. (Deut. 30:19)

Here God commands that all people are to choose life. Thus when faced with the opportunity to choose life, God desires for people to do so. God says that those choosing life are choosing that which is blessed, while those choosing death are choosing to act in opposition to God.

There are six things that the Lord hates,
seven that are an abomination to him:
haughty eyes, a lying tongue,
and hands that shed innocent blood, (Prov. 6:16-17)

The shedding of innocent blood is an act that brings the Lord's hatred. God does not desire for any person to kill another person unless in self-defense. Since God is the giver of life, God also determines what actions justify the taking of another human life. There is no action that the unborn can take, unless threatening the physical life of the mother, that would justify killing the unborn according to the Scripture.

Blessed are the peacemakers, for they shall be called sons
of God. (Matt. 5:9)

In this passage Jesus teaches about God's desire for people to adhere to a peaceful stance towards other people. This naturally applies to the unborn children as well.

But I say to you, Love your enemies and pray for those
who persecute you, (Matt. 5:44)

In this passage Jesus furthers the concept of acting peaceably toward other people by including even enemies in the group of people that are to be loved and treated kindly. It is not uncommon for people in today's society to characterize the unborn as an enemy of the mother who inhabits the mother's womb without permission. However, even if this were true, Jesus has called us as people to treat our enemies with love and it is the gospel of Jesus which provides the power to transform our feelings of animosity into love. We are therefore to treat the unborn with love even if we feel like we are being intruded upon by their presence.

Religion that is pure and undefiled before God, the Father, is this: to visit orphans and widows in their affliction, and to keep oneself unstained from the world. (Jas. 1:27)

This passage speaks to God's love for even the abandoned of the world. Widows have been abandoned through their spouses' deaths while orphans have lost their parents. Even in these circumstances, God affirms the worth of all human beings by commanding that proper conduct requires caring for the helpless. This can be extended to those who are dependent on others for their lives as well such as the unborn.

The Unborn Child is a Person from Conception

The following verses incorporate elements of the truth that God creates all life and that human life begins at conception. It should be understood that human life and personhood need to be treated synonymously to be consistent with the Scripture. This will become clear as the following passages are discussed.

Your hands fashioned and made me, and now you have destroyed me altogether. Remember that you have made me like clay; and will you return me to the dust? Did you not pour me out like milk and curdle me like cheese? You clothed me with skin and flesh, and knit me together with bones and sinews.

You have granted me life and steadfast love,
and your care has preserved my spirit. (Job 10:8-12)

This passage speaks to how God is the creator of life as well as the sustainer. When people try to intervene by taking another person's life they are trying to fill the role that is established for God alone. This is true from the moment of conception. Job recognized that God formed him in the womb and sustained his life. It follows that since God is the giver of life and forms each person, that God has a plan for each person. Although from God's perspective a person may have been known prior to their earthly conception, from the human perspective the person comes into being at the moment of conception when their unique physical instructions manifest.

Now the word of the Lord came to me, saying,
"Before I formed you in the womb I knew you,
and before you were born I consecrated you;
I appointed you a prophet to the nations."
Then I said, "Ah, Lord God! Behold, I do not know how
to speak, for I am only a youth." (Jer. 1:4-6)

Here in this passage the concept that God knows every single person prior to the person's physical conception is affirmed. The implication for this truth is that at the moment of conception a new human being is created that has worth, value, and purpose. Thus, God forms each individual person from conception onward. Just like with Jeremiah, each person is known to God prior to being formed in the womb. As God's creation, no one but God has the right to interfere with the life of the unborn child.

But when he who had set me apart before I was born, and
who called me by his grace, (Gal. 1:15)

Again in this NT passage God conveys that He is the one who determines certain aspects of life for people even prior to their being born. God sees the worth in all human beings, even those who are still living in the womb.

> *And Isaac prayed to the Lord for his wife, because she was*
> *barren. And the Lord granted his prayer, and Rebekah his*
> *wife conceived. The children struggled together within*
> *her, and she said, "If it is thus, why is this happening to*
> *me?" So she went to inquire of the Lord. And the Lord*
> *said to her,*
>
> > *"Two nations are in your womb,*
> > *and two peoples from within you shall be divided;*
> > *the one shall be stronger than the other,*
> > *the older shall serve the younger."*
>
> *When her days to give birth were completed, behold,*
> *there were twins in her womb. (Gen. 25:21-24)*

In this passage the Scripture indicates that it is the Lord that brings conception to pass and identifies Jacob and Esau as "children" while they are still in Rebekah's womb. Furthermore, the passage indicates that the Lord already knows what is going to transpire in the lives of both Jacob and Esau for many generations beyond them even prior to the time of their birth. This is a powerful passage that indicates that after children are conceived they are seen as fully human and valuable to God.

> *When men strive together and hit a pregnant woman, so*
> *that her children come out, but there is no harm, the one*
> *who hit her shall surely be fined, as the woman's husband*
> *shall impose on him, and he shall pay as the judges*
> *determine. But if there is harm, then you shall pay life for*
> *life, eye for eye, tooth for tooth, hand for hand, foot for*
> *foot, burn for burn, wound for wound, stripe for stripe.*
> *(Exo. 21:22-25)*

"The key passage in the hotly contested debate over the destruction of the human embryo or fetus is Exodus 21:22-25."[16] Exo. 21:22-25 has often been referred to as discussing miscarriage in the first case and abortion in the second (verses 22 and 23). However, Kaiser states that in both instances abortion is in view. He describes how there is a specific Hebrew word for miscarriage but that word is not utilized in this passage. Rather, the passage describes how if a woman's child is forced to come out then the perpetrator of the action that resulted in this must pay with his life. It holds up the standard penalty, a life for a life. So in verse 22 if no harm comes there is one penalty, but in verse 23 if harm occurs then the penalty is consistent with the taking of life. This passage illustrates how God views the unborn as human regardless of the state of development.

> *Behold, I was brought forth in iniquity,*
> *and in sin did my mother conceive me. (Psa. 51:5)*

In Psalm 51:5 David discusses his sin which existed as his mother conceived him. Bosgra describes the significance of this verse when he says, "Scripture attributes human sin not only to adults and children, but also to life in the womb. Yet Scripture never attributes human sin to either the male sperm or the female unfertilized ovum. Human sin does not exist in a vacuum. Where human sin exists, a human being exists. Thus, when destroying a pregnancy, man is ending a life created by God."[17]

> *For you formed my inward parts;*
> *you knitted me together in my mother's womb.*
> *I praise you, for I am fearfully and wonderfully made.*
> *Wonderful are your works;*
> *my soul knows it very well.*
> *My frame was not hidden from you,*
> *when I was being made in secret,*
> *intricately woven in the depths of the earth.*
> *Your eyes saw my unformed substance;*
> *in your book were written, every one of them,*
> *the days that were formed for me,*

when as yet there was none of them. (Psa. 139:13-16)

Just as in Gen. 25:21-24, this passage describes how God is the creator of life who forms each person in the womb from the time of conception. Additionally, God knows each person even prior to the time of their physical conception. God is truly the creator and sustainer of every human life and affirming the humanity and personhood of the unborn is affirming God's providential action in the lives of people.

Now the birth of Jesus Christ took place in this way. When his mother Mary had been betrothed to Joseph, before they came together she was found to be with child from the Holy Spirit. (Matt. 1:18)

But as he considered these things, behold, an angel of the Lord appeared to him in a dream, saying, "Joseph, son of David, do not fear to take Mary as your wife, for that which is conceived in her is from the Holy Spirit. She will bear a son, and you shall call his name Jesus, for he will save his people from their sins." (Matt. 1:20-21)

Jesus, being fully God and fully human, needed to go through the entire developmental process of what it means to be a human being. Thus, Jesus began His time on earth from the moment of conception. This should serve as further confirmation that from the moment of conception, God views each person as being fully human and possessing worth. Each earthly human life begins at the point of conception and continues until death.

...for he will be great before the Lord. And he must not drink wine or strong drink, and he will be filled with the Holy Spirit, even from his mother's womb. (Luke 1:15)

Again in this passage it is clear that prior to birth, John the Baptist was to be filled with the Holy Spirit. The Scripture teaches that only people can be filled so it can be concluded that John was human even before his birth.

> *In those days Mary arose and went with haste into the hill
> country, to a town in Judah, and she entered the house
> of Zechariah and greeted Elizabeth. And when Elizabeth
> heard the greeting of Mary, the baby leaped in her womb.
> And Elizabeth was filled with the Holy Spirit, and she
> exclaimed with a loud cry, "Blessed are you among
> women, and blessed is the fruit of your womb! And why
> is this granted to me that the mother of my Lord should
> come to me? For behold, when the sound of your greeting
> came to my ears, the baby in my womb leaped for joy.
> (Luke 1:39-44)*

This passage again demonstrates that the unborn is fully human
even prior to birth. John while still in the womb is referred to as a
"baby" and he even leapt for joy. Thus the unborn are persons from
conception and come to develop feelings and thoughts prior to birth.
Yet again, Scripture affirms the humanity of the unborn who should be
afforded full personhood and protection of the law.

> *...even as he chose us in him before the foundation of the
> world, that we should be holy and blameless before him.
> In love he predestined us for adoption as sons through
> Jesus Christ, according to the purpose of his will. (Eph.
> 1:4-5)*

This final passage further reiterates that God knows each and every
person prior to even the time that they are conceived here on earth.
Thus to not attribute full personhood from the point of conception
onward is to take a position that is inconsistent with that taken by God
and which is clearly revealed in Scripture.

It can be concluded as follows from the biblical data, that as for
abortion, no abortion except in the case of self-defense (the mother
will die, e.g., an ectopic pregnancy) is permissible. God is the creator

and sustainer of life. God knows how each person will be formed as well as what that person's life is going to be like prior to his or her conception. A view that attributes full personhood from the moment of conception is the view that is consistent with Scripture. Although the courts have ruled that human life begins when a child is born, the Bible establishes that life begins at conception. Since conception is an act of God and God determines who will conceive and when conception occurs, it is truly God's prerogative to make the determination in this matter.

Lastly, it should be noted that the New Testament makes no specific mention of abortion directly. However, some have suggested that there may be an implicit reference to abortion as the same word used to identify abortifacients in pagan writings of the same era, *pharmakeia*, is used in Gal. 5:20 and Rev. 9:21, 21:8, and 22:15 in the context of sexual immorality. Thus, the references in Galatians and Revelation, although not direct, appear to reject at least one major means of abortion in their rejection of drugs and poisons.[18] Although the method of killing is a lesser issue than the morality of killing, this information is still useful as some have argued that the OT test for adultery (Num. 5:11-31) involved using an abortifacient. In light of these NT passages this interpretation of the OT passage would seem to fail.

Abortion From The Time Of Constantine To The Industrial Revolution

Having now reviewed the scriptural data related to abortion it can be stated with certainty that up until about three hundred A.D. abortion was practiced, but it was never a practice that was condoned by those conforming their lives to God's Word, namely the Jews and Christians. Because of the revelation given by God, the Jews and Christians had clear insight into God's moral view of abortion. As such, they opposed abortion and ultimately the opposition that was raised eventually began to bear fruit. Having examined the Scriptural data, it is time to return to tracing how abortion has been perceived socially and legally from the fourth century A.D. to the present.

At the beginning of the fourth century, punishments for abortion and infanticide were prescribed at the Council of Elvira. This coincided with the Christianization of the Roman Empire in 313 A.D. under Constantine. What resulted from the Christian faith being thrust upon the empire was a situation in which many people now became Christian due to the society or culture they were a part of, rather than by their faith in Christ. This situation is not too different from what is observed in the United States today. The result of the Christianization under Constantine was that there was an increase in the practice of abortion in the church due to the pagan influence of so many new church members.[19]

Towards the end of the fourth century abortion was still seen as not only wrong but an act of disobedience against God. In A.D. 374, Basil of Caesarea wrote a statement about abortion that revealed his view that abortion is a crime as well as a sin. He did not see abortion as an unforgivable sin, but that abortion had to be considered as a serious disregard for human life and was thus equated with murder. Although he believed the sin of abortion was serious and would be judged by God, like murder it could be forgiven by God's grace.[20]

This view of abortion, the termination of a life created by God, considered morally wrong and an act of murder, was also held by the Church Fathers until the fifth century. Ambrose and John Chrysostom both held to this view as did Augustine. Augustine however took a position similar to the early Alexandrian rabbinical view that differentiated between the formed and unformed fetus. Augustine saw destruction of the fetus at any stage as immoral but held that only after the fetus was formed could it be deemed to be murder. Despite this, his general stance was one which valued all life whether actual or potential.

It is obvious that the Christian teaching related to abortion has always been against abortion in general. The Church Fathers were in agreement on this, and the church as a whole continued to hold this position for centuries. Even when the level of immorality assigned to the act of abortion based on the various developmental stages of the child was espoused, the church never endorsed or approved of abortion. It was always seen as immoral and an act against God.

It should be noted that both pagans and Christians alike have criticized abortion for the last two thousand years. It is interesting that the point of agreement between the two groups involves the sense that abortion should not be performed because a woman feels like it or for her convenience. Historically, both pagans and Christians alike have criticized the use of abortion as an effort to conceal sexual immorality or as a means of birth control. Additionally, both groups also expressed concern for the safety of the woman who chose to attempt to abort her child. But what set the Christians who opposed abortion apart from the pagans who likewise opposed abortion, was the Christian concern for the unborn child. Pagans opposed to abortion never entertained the rights of the unborn child. Christian opponents to abortion, however, viewed the unborn child as an independent living being, God's creation, and thus entitled to be protected like any other person. In this regard, little has changed during the last two thousand years between the Christian and pagan perspectives.

Gorman succinctly summarizes the position of the Christian church from its beginning to today when he states,

> *The earliest Christian ethic, from Jesus to Constantine, can be described as a consistent pro-life ethic. It was in favor of human life regardless of age, nationality or social standing. It pleaded for the poor, the weak, women, children and the unborn. This pro-life ethic discarded hate in favor of love, war in favor of peace, oppression in favor of justice, bloodshed in favor of life. The Christian's response to abortion was one important aspect of this consistent pro-life ethic. Rooted in Jewish love for life and hatred of bloodshed, it developed a specific Christian character as part of early Christian holistic discipleship. To follow Jesus was to forsake bloodshed.*[21]

The Christian church has held its prohibition against abortion since its beginning. However, some have argued that abortion at the early stages of a child's development is not as serious in God's eyes. This concept continued to surface at times and was the basis for the Catholic Church declaring in 1591 that abortion before quickening was only a venial sin and carried no penalties.[22] It must be noted, this position fails to take into consideration that the Christian prohibition against taking human life is not based in the value of a life per se, but rather on the conviction that the life is not ours to take. Rather, all life is seen as belonging to God the Creator. As such, as human beings and bearers of God's image, all people are worthy of and in need of protection and love regardless of their developmental age.

Abortion In The Modern Era

Similar to the early rabbinical schools of thought, a distinction in the early development of a child was adopted in the United States. A distinction was made between a child prior to and after quickening. Quickening was the time at which the baby could be felt to move, or roughly during the fourth month of pregnancy. Prior to the mid-1800s, abortion was legal in the United States as long as it was performed prior to quickening. In fact, abortion services were even advertised.[23] But the sentiment began to change in the mid-1800s.

In the 1850s the American Medical Association launched an effort to outlaw abortion. As a result, abortion became illegal except in circumstances where the physician deemed it medically necessary.[24] This was accomplished when the American Medical Association commissioned an investigation into abortion rates while simultaneously promoting abortion as dangerous by using provocative terms such as antenatal infanticide. "By the end of the Civil War, most states had outlawed abortion, and the situation persisted well into the 20th century."[25]

Although the implication by many historians is that anti-abortion legislation was enacted to create an environment where physicians retained control of medical procedures, there were certainly other forces at play. Some argue that another reason why anti-abortion laws were being passed in the mid-1800s, was the social fear that due to the high birth rate of the newly arriving immigrant families, that ultimately if abortion were not banned for Anglo women, the immigrant population would come to predominate the Anglo population given the lower birth rates of the native Anglo-Saxon women.[26] In addition to these political and social reasons, it should not be forgotten that the church continued to view abortion as morally wrong. This reality cannot be discounted as the Christian religion continued to impact society and individuals during this time in our history.

By the late 1800s, the early feminist movement was taking shape. The first feminists in the nineteenth century were all against abortion because of their belief that all human beings have worth. They described abortion as child murder and infanticide. In part, as a result of the original feminist movement, laws were enacted against abortion. One such piece of legislation was the 1873 Comstock Act. This federal law, in addition to numerous similar state laws, outlawed the mailing of contraceptive and abortion related implements and information as they were deemed to be obscene and immoral. Offenders faced imprisonment and fines for violations of the Comstock Laws. Until 1973 abortions in the United States were prohibited under the Comstock Laws which had been enacted a century earlier. In an ironic twist, the laws preventing abortion remained for nearly a century until the feminists of the 1960s and 1970s sought to overturn the very laws that their predecessors had passed by their advocacy. This occurred with the ruling in *Roe v. Wade*.[27]

Certainly the feminist movement had changed during its first century. What began as a life affirming movement of promoting equal value for all human beings transformed into a demand by the modern feminists for freedom and a near exaltation of women. Women were no longer seeking recognition as equal in worth as women but rather sought recognition as equal in all ways to men. Mary Ann Glendon astutely describes an interesting phenomena that distinguished this new feminism from its original roots when she says, "But the feminism of the 1970s was different. What made it different was a puzzling combination of two things that do not ordinarily go together: anger against men and promiscuity; man-hating and man-chasing."[28]

Certainly in the 1970s, society had changed from a century prior. Women held differing roles than their mothers and grandmothers before them had even dreamed of possessing. Vast educational and career opportunities had opened up and were readily available to women at all ages for the first time. But these changes did not come without consequences. With women who now chose to spend more time outside of the home, the family was subjected to enormous social, economic, cultural, and ideological pressures unlike any known previously.[29]

One such pressure on the family involved the deinstitutionaliza-tion of the Christian religion in the country. As the government passed legislation suggesting that religion was a private matter and not one to be commingled with politics, work, and education, religion began to take a back seat to other social forces. As a result, secular and political leaders began to dictate a new set of gender roles as well as a new morality. Ostrom describes how even the view of sin, or conduct that is in opposition to God, has become secularized as a result of the dein-stitutionalization of Christianity.

> *Much of what in the distant past had been called sin, was labeled crime from the middle ages on. Then under the influence of Freud in the early 1900s and the evolution of modern psychiatry and psychology, sin became illness. Society's progression from the religious to the secular made people reluctant about moralizing. People seemed to take to heart the admonition "judge not that ye may be judged (Math. 7:1)."[30]*

Ostrom further describes the result of the religious being replaced by the secular as manifesting in a societal mandate for individuals to become self-absorbed as the masters of their own destinies. Thus the baby boomers came to be known as the "me generation" due to the rampant rise in narcissism which took the form of pursuing self-reali-zation and self-fulfillment.

This rise in self-absorption took place at a time when society was undergoing tremendous social changes. Candace Crandall notes how this self-absorption and the social pressures of the 1960s ultimately came to manifest when she says,

> *In the 1960s, the nation was caught up in the turmoil of three great social movements: civil rights, with its emphasis on bringing about sweeping political change via the courts; feminism, with its promise to empower the*

victims of very real social and economic injustice; and environmentalism, which had fostered widespread hysteria with warnings of an imminent population disaster. The point at which the tenets of these three movements converged was abortion.[31]

The result of abortion becoming the focal point of the various social pressures led to a change of guard in terms of who would be allowed to serve as gate keeper regarding childbirth. Although the medical establishment had dominance over childbearing and abortion for the century from 1850 to 1950, things were going to rapidly change. When physicians served as gate keepers, a woman with money had access to abortion for practically any reason through a physician but the decision was ultimately for the physician to decide not the woman. In the 1960s, this changed as abortion was legalized and the decisional process was shifted to the woman from the physician. This also led to a significant increase in the number of abortions that were performed.[32]

As the focus on the self grew deep roots and began to spread, the concept of each person possessing a right to choice emerged. This culture of choice, which began in the 1960s and certainly was flourishing by the 1970s, has impacted nearly every element of American life. Erika Bachiochi describes how freedom of choice or consent works fairly well in the free market economy but "operates rather like a wrecking crew upon marriage, family, and relations between a mother and her unborn child."[33] The increase in abortion and divorce rates speak to the veracity of this observation. It was reported that the nuclear family, a foundational societal institution, had fallen to a point where under a quarter of all households were thus composed, according to the 2000 Census data. This decrease in the percentage of nuclear families was observed to have fallen from approximately fifty percent of all families being considered nuclear families in 1960.[34]

Bachiochi discusses how as people have adopted the current societal philosophy of freedom of choice that what has resulted is a sense that they are only obligated when they want to be obligated. She describes how many Americans still believe the mother should not be obligated to protect or care for a child in the womb even though seventy-four percent of Americans believe that having an abortion is taking a human life. Only when a mother chooses to become pregnant does any obligation follow. As such, this culture of choice has made its impact in the personal realm of marriage, family, and pregnancy.[35]

Perhaps freedom of choice would not be detrimental if exercised within the proper framework. But this does not seem to be the case. Rather than operating in a rational manner in accord with a universal morality, the contemporary culture of choice tends to rely upon passion to govern decisions. Just as passions change, decisions change. A choice is only binding as long as the person feels it should be binding. Certainly this mindset has an impact upon the children who have yet to be born. The women who choose to have an abortion generally do so because they are fearful, not because they have fully weighed the logical and moral implications of the various options. When fears related to being unable to care for a child due to financial difficulty, a lack of maturity, a lack of time, or a lack of support arise, passions can steer a woman towards alleviating her fears of child rearing by having an abortion.

Yet, giving people the freedom to choose without constraint as a legal construct leads to some rather significant contradictions in the law, especially concerning the unborn child. Bachiochi cites a Minnesota law where a child at ten weeks of age can be considered the victim of murder if intentionally killed by the father. However, in the circumstance where this same ten week old child is intentionally aborted by the mother, there would be no legal ramifications. Rather, the mother's killing of the child would be seen as a product of women's liberation.[36]

This author agrees with Bachiochi who sees the current construal of the right to choice as being the right to create one's own reality. It is analogous to making gods of people who now determine for themselves the great questions of existence such as what does it mean to be human, to possess value, or to worship God. Furthermore, these determinations are subject to change at will depending on how the person is feeling. A woman can choose whether the child she is carrying is a human person deserving of protection or not. Based upon the woman's choice alone, not science or reason, the unborn's status as a human person is determined under current American law.

The culture we live in today is not that of two generations ago. Over the last forty years a radical shift has occurred which has left everyone, but especially the weak and defenseless, more vulnerable and without protection. Our society has become a culture inconsistent with the very values upon which the country was formed and as Bachiochi says,

> *It is a culture that employs a contractual, consumerist mentality when it comes to marriage and family generally, and pregnancy specifically...It teaches that happiness depends on making choices according to one's own desire or pleasure, or one's own (often fear-based) assessment of one's needs. The age-old notion that good character is built upon good choices made in the midst of difficult circumstances has been replaced by indifference to attaining good character at all...the culture of choice has exalted the impulses of human will and passions over truth and reason.[37]*

The promotion of choice over reason and the feminist push to define equality as equal in all ways has led to tremendous changes in how women contend with trying to fit into their very own lives. To be pregnant is now seen as being on par with having a disability as it impairs one's ability to function in the workforce or to financially support a family. Women who might have a desire to be a wife and mother must swim upstream against the current which proclaims that being a housewife is equivalent with being enslaved and oppressed. It appears that a woman's unique feminine identity has now been displaced by an identity, which appears for all intents and purposes, as the historical masculine identity. Men are still men, but now women must be men also if they are to reconcile their sense of self with society's image of womanhood. This sociological factor in turn bears upon the psychological elements of self and identity which makes abortion seem like a necessity for a woman to maintain her very identity.

In addition to the radical change in the feminine identity, Dr. Will

Ford describes how cultural mores were changing in the 1960s and the impact that this has had on society in general and women in particular. As the popular culture began in the 1960s to shape the perspective of the American people through music and entertainment, the prior era's moral sense that espoused monogamy, self-restraint, and familial obligation was dispatched. Replacing the traditional moral values was a social climate that supported both self-gratification and sexual freedom which had not been known to such an extent previously in American society. As a result, the perspective that it was wrong to restrain the self from engaging in pleasure became pervasive.[38] But this posed an especially difficult problem for women. How can a woman have unrestrained sexual relations when the result of sexual behavior oftentimes is pregnancy which impairs future sexual freedom? Although contraceptive advances seemed to be part of the solution, it was no panacea and pregnancy continued to occur. Rather than change the conduct and recognize that the moral departure was the problem, people decided that rather than change their conduct, they needed to retain their freedoms at any cost.

Hence the first rumblings of all-out war on the unborn truly began in the United States. Now as political liberalism has taken hold and permeated all aspects of the American psyche, the importance of individual rights and pursuing happiness based upon one's own individual morality has resulted in a societal circumstance where truth claims exist in large part independent of one another. Even though there is an underlying belief that the government should take a neutral stance toward individuals in the choices they make governing their happiness, society has never been completely consistent in this regard. The government has outlawed polygamy and slavery which certainly imposed a moral standard on the populace as a whole. Additionally, by allowing for abortion to be available, the government has again imposed a set of moral standards, namely that ending the life of the unborn in the womb is acceptable. Thus the government cannot be truly neutral, for to endorse one position is to negate the other. Laws pertaining to moral issues are never neutral, they always represent a particular moral stance. Hence, as the legal decisions made by the government are subsequently examined, the government's moral stance will be unveiled.

In summary, the socio-political feminist movement which began as a pro-life movement morphed into the pro-choice movement. With the rise of feminism in the 1960s, abortion access became a natural outgrowth as women saw the need to have control and an independent authority over their role, even that of motherhood. True freedom for women meant having the decision over whether to become a parent or not.[39]

Recently however, a new wave of feminists are beginning to appear. Women who realize that the feminism of unrestrained choice is not a feminism that ultimately is pro-woman. Now many pro-life feminists believe abortion devalues motherhood and threatens the feminine values of intimacy, nurturance, community, and care.[40] The pendulum is swinging back towards the original tenets of feminism where the belief that child rearing is punishment for choosing to have sexual intercourse is being flatly rejected. This current feminist movement sees childbearing as uniquely a female task, and thus must be honored and protected if women in general are to be honored, protected, and valued.

Legal Decisions Impacting Abortion In The United States Today

A near reversal in the way abortion was treated legislatively occurred from 1873 to 1973. Abortion went from being an illegal procedure in 1873 to a procedure regulated less than the pulling of teeth by 1973. This change in the legislative treatment did not occur gradually. Rather over the course of a decade, beginning in the 1960s, a complete transformation occurred.

By 1965 all fifty states had enacted legislation which specified that performing an abortion or attempting to have an abortion were deemed to be felonious activities unless the abortion was performed to save the mother's life. By 1973, a number of jurisdictions had adopted far more permissive abortion laws which granted the ability to perform an abortion to licensed physicians, generally only in accredited hospitals, who determined that the pregnancy would seriously injure the physical or mental health of the mother. As the mental health provision was included, so was the exception to the prohibition on abortion in cases of rape or incest. Additionally, abortion was allowed for situations where the child was determined to have problems which would result in being born with significant physical or mental defects. The late 1960s and early 1970s marked a time in abortion legislation where the laws were allowing for abortion in cases where the pregnancy was deemed to be detrimental in some way to the mother as well as society.[41]

In *Griswold v. Connecticut*, 381 US 479 (1965), the United States Supreme Court struck down a Connecticut statute that prohibited the use of contraceptives and the counseling of people to use contraceptives. This case involved Estelle Griswold who was the executive director of the Planned Parenthood League of Connecticut and Dr. C. Lee Buxton who was a doctor and Yale Medical School professor who both were arrested under the Connecticut statute and found to be guilty of being accessories to providing contraception. Each was fined and they subsequently appealed their case which was ultimately heard by the Supreme Court. The Court found that there is a right to privacy that exists in the marital bedroom, and that such privacy extends to the choices made within the marital bedroom, including the right of married people to use contraceptives. This finding resulted in the Court ruling that the Connecticut law was void as it violated the privacies created by and protected under the constitution. This decision began to lay the foundation which would ultimately culminate in the Court's ruling in *Roe v. Wade*.

In *Eisenstadt v. Baird*, 405 US 438 (1972), the Supreme Court struck down a Massachusetts statute that prevented the dissemination of contraceptives to single individuals as the statute was deemed to not apply equally to married and unmarried individuals. This ruling increased the availability of contraceptive products to all people concluding that unmarried people have the same right to contraception as married people. This served as a spring board for *Roe v. Wade* as the Court in *Eisenstadt* said people have a right to choose to have non-procreative sex. When *Griswold* and *Eisenstadt* are paired it creates an environment which mandates contraceptive access to all people while simultaneously stating that people have a right to engage in non-procreative sex. The Court could not have made it any clearer that it was supporting the concept that the constitution provided for the right to engage in sexual relations by the people without having to consider any consequences of such sexual behavior. *Roe v. Wade* was a logical next step.

Before looking at the facts involved in the *Roe* decision, the consequences of what this decision meant for the people of America, both those who were born as well as those who were not yet born, should be understood. Some have tried to argue that prior to *Roe* that the number of illegal abortions was roughly equivalent to the number of legal abortions after *Roe*. However, Wilcox provides evidence to the contrary as, "...the overall trend in abortion numbers and rates increased from 23,000 in 1969 (pre-*Roe*) to about 1.6 million in 1990."[42] This is a seventy fold increase. In fact, there have been more deaths due to abortion since abortion was legalized in 1973 than there have been from all American wars combined. Approximately 1.2 million people have died in combat from the Revolutionary war through Vietnam. However on an annual basis, 1.5 million abortions occur in the United States alone. "It amounts to one baby being killed in America every twenty seconds, twenty-four hours each day." This is despite the Judeo-Christian principles which emphasize the sanctity of life and upon which the United States was founded.[43]

Now, it is not just the pro-life authors who indicate that *Roe* led to a dramatic increase in abortions. Even the pro-choice authors generally concede that the Court's ruling led to a significant increase in the number of abortions. Runkle describes how the 1973 Supreme Court legalization of abortion in *Roe v. Wade* has led to a rapid increase in the number of abortions that were performed. She says that the number of abortions has stabilized at around one and a half million abortions per year in the United States.[44]

The landmark case, *Roe v. Wade*, 410 US 113 (1973), can be thought of as the open declaration of war in the United States against people in the womb. Additionally, *Roe*'s companion case, *Doe v. Bolton*, 410 US 179, (1973) swung open the flood gates giving women the choice to abort their unborn child for virtually any reason for the entire nine months of pregnancy.

The issue in *Roe* was the Texas statute that prevented termination of pregnancy for a reason other than to save the life of the mother.

This case involved a pregnant woman, *Roe*, who brought a class action challenging the Texas statutes that limited abortion to circumstances necessary to save the mother's life. Although at the time the case went to the Supreme Court, *Roe* was no longer pregnant, the Court found she still had standing as to bring her suit.

Ultimately the Court ruled that the Texas statutes were unconstitutional. The Court stated that *Roe* possessed the right to terminate her pregnancy and that, "Appellant would discover this right in the concept of personal 'liberty' embodied in the Fourteenth Amendment's Due Process Clause; or in personal, marital, familial, and sexual privacy said to be protected by the Bill of Rights or its penumbras."[45]

> *The Court argued for why restricting abortion was improper when it stated,*
>
> *Maternity, or additional offspring, may force upon the woman a distressful life and future. Psychological harm may be imminent. Mental and physical health may be taxed by child care. There is also the distress, of all concerned, associated with the unwanted child, and there is the problem of bringing a child into a family already unable, psychologically and otherwise, to care for it. In other cases, as in this one, the additional difficulties and continuing stigma of unwed motherhood may be involved. All these are factors the woman and her responsible physician necessarily will consider in consultation.*[46]

The Court discussed how if the unborn child met criteria for "personhood" then the child would be protected under the Fourteenth Amendment. However, the Court then proceeded to discuss how they did not believe the Fourteenth Amendment entertained the unborn in defining persons. This was the Court's attempt at espousing the double speak necessary to justify their ruling. The Court proceeded to say that, "There has always been strong support for the view that life does not begin until live birth…"[47] and that "In short, the unborn have never been recognized in the law as persons in the whole sense."[48]

Strangely, the Court then proceeded to discuss the State's interest in fulfilling its obligation to protect all people. The Court reasoned that the State's interest in the unborn child did not become "compelling" until the time of viability stating that "the fetus then presumably has the capability of meaningful life outside the mother's womb."[49] Here the Court seems to waffle on how life is even defined by first determining that full life does not begin until birth and that the law has not entertained the unborn historically while simultaneously advancing the argument that if the unborn could live outside the womb then the state may, but is not required to, entertain the unborn as people deserving and entitled to protections.

The case of *Roe v. Wade* decided in 1973, effectively established that a woman can have an abortion for any reason she deems fit through the first six months of her pregnancy as the Court said the woman has a right to make choices about her body and her pregnancy. This ruling made it unconstitutional for a state to prohibit abortion at any time prior to viability for the unborn child. Generally this period was extended through the second trimester or approximately the first five to six months of pregnancy. In fact, a woman now has the constitutionally guaranteed right, according to the Court, to terminate a pregnancy prior to viability.

For the last three months when the unborn child is deemed to be viable, the state has the right to restrict abortion but is not obligated to do so. Those states which have enacted legislative restrictions during the third trimester to allow for abortion only to protect maternal health, tend to define health so broadly that effectively there is no restriction at all. A woman who claims she needs an abortion to preserve her emotional well-being can have an abortion performed and still be within the guidelines of the law. In essence, *Roe* created a situation where women can have an abortion on demand.

Although *Roe* did create legal abortion for the duration of a woman's pregnancy, it was the ruling in *Doe v. Bolton*, 410 US 179 that truly made abortion on demand for the duration of a woman's pregnancy a reality. *Doe* removed a number of the restrictions that Georgia had in place to insure that abortions were only performed to protect the life of the mother. Georgia's statutes were enacted in an effort to protect the interests of the woman as well as the unborn child. The Court found these restrictions to be unconstitutional and saw them as unduly restrictive. The ruling in *Doe* indicated that legislative efforts to protect the life of the unborn child were now doomed to fail.[50]

The primary significance of the ruling in *Doe* was the Court's defining health as well being. This is a far more general definition of health and thus women are able to have their abortions justified for nearly any reason throughout the entire nine months of their pregnancy. Even though the Court's ruling created a situation where abortion on demand is an option throughout the entire nine months of pregnancy, the American public has never supported this.[51] As a result of the rulings in *Roe* and *Doe* the pro-choice advocates are able to advance arguments which on the surface have the appearance of legitimacy. However, under scrutiny even these arguments fail due to internal self-contradiction. Claire, a pro-choice advocate and author, puts forth that it "Is up to pro-choice advocates to get the message out that *abortion is not murder*."[52]

Claire makes the argument that abortion is not murder because murder requires the unlawful killing of another human being with forethought. She argues that since abortion is now legal, it cannot be murder. She also argues that the belief that the unborn child is a human being from the moment of conception cannot be substantiated by any scientific or biologic evidence. "It is important that pro-choice advocates understand that terminating a pregnancy is killing something that's *human* and *alive*, but not yet 'a baby.'"[53]

Claire argues that of the three elements necessary to define abortion as murder (premeditation, unlawfulness, and a human being) that only premeditation can reasonably be applied to abortion. She makes this claim because abortion is legal and that although it is killing, it is not the killing of a person as long as the abortion occurs prior to twenty-eight weeks of gestation. Claire arrives at this developmental age by relying on experts who claim that an unborn child cannot feel pain prior to twenty-eight weeks development. Somehow the assumption that feeling pain as the defining characteristic in humanness has been slipped into Claire's argument. She concludes that abortion kills the potential for the unborn child to develop but does not kill an actual human being.

Claire further argues that an abortion in the third trimester may not be murder even though it is past the time of viability and past the time the unborn child can feel pain. To determine if abortion would be murder at this developmental stage would require evaluating the situation to see if the mother had a lawful cause to kill the child, such as her life being threatened. Claire's position takes on another unique twist as she advocates for the right to terminate a severely crippled or fatally ill child during the third trimester. However, she desires that this procedure not be called abortion but rather euthanasia. Claire's argument for abortion illustrates that the thinking required to justify abortion likewise leads to infanticide and euthanasia.

Claire's reasoning is internally contradictory and she struggles to justify her position. At one moment she argues that science and biology cannot substantiate that an unborn child from the moment of conception is a human being but then she proceeds to say that what is being killed is a human and alive but somehow not yet a baby. Euthanasia means Claire deems killing acceptable when it serves what is deemed to be purposeful. Thus Claire's argument regarding abortion is really an argument for euthanasia of unwanted people in general cloaked in the context of abortion. *Roe* has certainly opened the door for attempts at such argumentation as Claire espouses.

If abortion remained illegal then many of the arguments attempting to justify abortion would not even be considered by the vast majority of the population. Stanley Hauerwas also draws this conclusion when he states, "But in our day the moral consensus has disintegrated in a number of significant respects: we no longer have agreement on the value of human life, or on such basic social institutions as marriage and the family, or for that matter on the meaning of being human."[54]

It has thus been accurately said that on "January 22, 1973 the closely related decisions of *Roe v. Wade* and *Doe v. Bolton* the U.S. Supreme Court used its judicial power to impose on our nation an abortion law which was more permissive than that of any other Western nation."[55] The effects of these rulings continue to impact the social, political, legal, moral, and spiritual functioning of our nation.

Is abortion just an issue that affects women? It would appear that the Court has concluded as much despite the fact that pregnancy does not occur except in cases where both a man and woman contribute. In *Planned Parenthood of Central Missouri v. Danforth*, 428 US 52 (1976), the Supreme Court revisited the abortion issue by considering prospective fathers' rights in the area of abortion. This case challenged the Missouri statutes that required spousal notification before a woman could undergo an abortion procedure. The Court ruled that women have a right to make a unilateral decision about whether they desire to abort or carry a pregnancy to term as husbands cannot have the right to veto when even the states do not have such authority.[56]

Thus, men are placed in the situation where they are disempowered regarding the outcome of their child. They are removed from the decision making process which will determine if their child will even be allowed to live. Men are compelled to be financially responsible to the child if a woman chooses to have the child, but they have no say in the child's life for the first nine months. For men who desire to have the child they are at the mercy of the woman who may choose to abort the child and leave the man traumatized and helpless to do anything to save the life of his child.

In *Webster v. Reproductive Health Services*, 492 US 490 (1989), the court rejected *Roe*'s trimester breakdown as well as the claim that the state only has interest in the prenatal life after viability.[57] This ruling appeared to allow the state to have greater ability to regulate abortion than was previously thought under *Roe*. The Missouri statute had in its preamble that human life began at conception and thus it was necessary to evaluate viability rather than just accept a predefined time period such as the trimester system. This case also allowed the state to impose restrictions on the use of state funds and facilities for abortion procedures.

This next case further appeared to weaken the rigid position that was established in *Roe*. In *Casey v. Planned Parenthood*, 505 US 833 (1992), the Court reaffirmed that the states' interest in the unborn child begins at viability. Just as in *Webster* the Court deemed that the trimester time demarcation was too rigid.[58] Rather the Court acknowledged that technological changes since the time of the *Roe* ruling had dropped the time of viability to around twenty-two weeks. As such, the Court still held to the basic premise in *Roe* which guaranteed a woman the ability to terminate her pregnancy prior to viability.

However, the Court also affirmed that the state had the right to impose reasonable requirements such as a twenty-four hour waiting period and proper informed consent. Thus *Casey* marked a period in time where the states' rights to protect the unborn were beginning to be weighed against the woman's privacy rights regarding her pregnancy. Additionally, by discussing how the time of viability was lowered due to medical technology, the Court opened the door for future changes regarding even earlier viability associated with advances in medical technology. It is conceivable that viability could one day occur at conception and thus *Casey* may someday be used to eliminate abortion completely.

In *Stenberg v. Carhart*, 530 US 914 (2000), the Supreme Court struck down a state statute that banned partial-birth abortion.[59] This was significant as partial-birth abortions take place when the physician partially delivers the live child and then applies a procedure which kills the child. The Court ruled that the Nebraska statute under review did not have an exception to protect the life of the mother and thus was unconstitutional. Furthermore, the Court upheld the right of the mother to abort her child as they had previously ruled in *Roe* and *Casey*.

In 2002 President Bush passed the "Born-Alive Infants Protection Act," which requires that any child who survives an abortion attempt be afforded all the protections of the law that apply to any other postnatal human being.[60] This was a significant piece of legislation as it afforded children all the rights of personhood immediately upon birth even if that birth was induced in an attempt at abortion. Previously, those children born in failed abortion attempts were often left to die and were not afforded the rights of personhood.

The next year in 2003, President Bush signed into law the Partial-Birth Abortion Ban Act and it was upheld by the Supreme Court in *Gonzales v. Carhart*, 550 US 124 (2007).[61] This legislation was found to be constitutional as it focused primarily on a method of abortion and not on preventing a woman from having an abortion. Thus it differed from the statute under review in *Stenberg v. Carhart* which the Supreme Court had invalidated in part because the statute was not sufficiently clear in specifying the method of abortion.

After the ruling in *Gonzalez* many states began to enact legislation to regulate abortion. Laws have been passed that outlaw abortion after twenty weeks of development as this is now the age where it is believed that the unborn child can feel pain and perhaps the child has become viable. However, opponents of these laws cite that viability of the unborn does not occur until at least twenty-one weeks and likely closer to twenty-four weeks. Additionally a number of states have passed laws requiring women to receive ultrasound procedures prior to an abortion where the woman is required to view the image of the child and listen to the heartbeat. So far, these laws have held up as meeting constitutional standards. It is possible that the Supreme Court will have to revisit the issue of viability again given their position in *Roe* that the state has the right to begin exercising its rights to protect the interests of the unborn child at the time of viability.

From The Courts To The Social Arena

Having an understanding of the legal foundation for the status of abortion allows the social and political climate to be better understood. It is particularly interesting that Americans tend to be more politically and socially affiliated in their stance on abortion than they are in terms of religion. Gorman describes how modern-day Christians fall into both the pro-life and pro-choice camps. He states that neither side really hears the arguments of the other side. In Gorman's conceptualization, the challenge of the abortion debate is that the pro-life side emphasizes the value of life while the pro-choice side emphasizes the value of freedom.[62] Gorman's analysis further reveals that indeed it is not the church that people are turning to in order to structure their lives but rather the social and political movements of the day. Hence, personal rights, a construct developed in the political and legal realms of discourse, become more influential than the tenets of the various religions.

Thus as Americans seek to find meaning in life and embrace the socio-political values of the day which include tolerance, individualism, and freedom, the public debate over legalizing abortion continues. Since the Supreme Court ruling in *Roe v. Wade* legalized abortion, the practice of abortion has now become an accepted practice based on the standard that what is lawful is acceptable. Hence in today's society, the majority of Americans believe that abortion should be legal in some form but there is still significant disagreement about which circumstances justify abortion.[63] Despite the disagreements, "Abortion is incredibly common; 45% of all women of reproductive age in the U.S. have had one."[64]

As moral relativism has swept through the modern culture like a wildfire, people's views on abortion have been impregnated with a relativistic nature. "Many people see relativism as necessary for promoting tolerance, nonjudgmentalism, and inclusiveness, for they think if one believes one's moral position is correct and others' incorrect, one is close-minded and intolerant."[65] It is now no longer popular to hold a view that contends that there are certain behaviors that people ought and ought not to do. This relativistic philosophy has permeated the thinking in all areas, but in the realm of abortion it reduces the choice of protecting the unborn to a mere preference. Beckwith describes this astutely when he describes how moral relativism has left the people of our country with the perspective that we all can determine for ourselves what is right and wrong. Hence, moral relativism promotes the view that "… when it comes to questions of morality, there is no absolute or objective right and wrong; moral rules are merely personal preferences and/or the result of one's cultural, sexual, or ethnic orientation. So choosing an abortion, like choosing an automobile, a vacation spot, or dessert, is merely a matter of preference."[66]

Relativism suffers from the same problems as other subjective approaches to defining morality and reality. Mark Hanna describes the fundamental flaw in relativism when he states,

If one is a subjectivist, he claims that "truth" and "reality" are the products of individual minds. Although there are many versions of subjectivism, they all agree that if there is an extrasubjective reality, it cannot be known. Either the mind is limited to its own contents or in its encounter with an ostensibly external world, it "imposes" its own structures on it so that what it knows is essentially the mind's creation.

In proffering this theory, however, subjectivists implicitly

> *deny it. For they tacitly claim that this is reality and that they know this truth about reality. This state of affairs, therefore, is exempted from being a creation of the mind or merely intrasubjective. And this arbitrary exemption is the self-destructive inconsistency that robs subjectivism of the power to oppose Christianity – or anything else, for that matter.*[67]

Despite the inherent problems with relativism, it is because of this relativistic philosophy that authors such as Runkle can suggest that men can best support their pregnant partners by taking the position that it "Is important to accept her role as the decision maker right now [regarding the pregnancy] and to give her as much emotional support as you can."[68] This is consistent with a relativistic position that suggests that only the woman herself can determine what the right thing to do is as each person must decide what is true. Additionally this is consistent with the feminist perspective that discourages women from looking to their male partners for guidance but to strive to be solely independent in decision making. Since the current legal situation does not recognize the father of a child as having any rights until the child is born, pro-choice feminists such as Runkle feel justified in relegating the fathers of the unborn to a peripheral role.

Yet Runkle's position is not that different from the general non-Christian view of societal freedom which polarizes freedom and determinism. In other words, Americans have adopted the belief that there should be an end to compulsion by others. This is unlike the historic Christian view of freedom which views freedom as the freedom from sin and the subsequent bondage that results. Hence, freedom viewed from a historic Christian perspective is tied to the deliverance found only in the relationship with Jesus Christ.[69] Yet the historic Christian view is not even seen as valid in this day and age. Hauerwas argues that the pro-life position cannot prevail in the current American culture because the political considerations of our culture have shaped what we determine to be moral. Our culture tends to take the position that any religious conviction invalidates a public view. "As a result the Christian prohibition of abortion appears as an irrational prejudice of religious people who cannot argue it on a secular, rational basis."[70]

Those debating the legality of abortion, especially those who advocate being able to choose to have an abortion, attempt to reduce the discussion to a matter of personal preference or subjective opinion. However, those opposed to abortion understand the argument as a moral argument. They recognize that morality calls for the law to take a stand on what people ought to do and what they ought not to do. When viewing abortion as a subjective preference the humanity of the unborn plays very little into the decision. However, when viewing abortion as a moral argument, the determination of what is moral is grounded in how the unborn child as a human being ought to be treated.

To further add to the confusion over what is moral is the confusion found in the church, historically the place people could go to find out what morality entailed. Today there are over two thousand religions derived from Christianity in the United States, which makes it very difficult to find a common belief regarding abortion within the Christian faith as it appears that all views are acceptable somewhere. In fact, Claire reports that she interviewed many clergymen who acknowledged there were circumstances that might lead to the necessity for moral compromise such as rape or incest. "If your congregation doesn't think as you do, 'shop around' buying one that does. There you will get the support you need during your abortion dilemma."[71] To make matters even worse, few Christian churches and denominations are holding to the historic doctrines which have been held for hundreds of years. Rather, the beliefs seem to be rapidly changing as of late along with the culture. As such, the church is looking more like the secular culture and this only contributes to the moral confusion which prevails in society today.

As Hunter opines,

> ...even the most optimistic assessment would lead one to conclude that Christianity in America is not only marginalized as a culture but it is also a very weak culture. For all of the vitality and all of the good intention among Christian believers, the whole (in terms of its influence

in the larger political economy of cultural production) is significantly less than the sum of its parts. And thus the idea that American Christianity could influence the larger culture in ways that are healthy and humane is, for the time being, doubtful.[72]

He further says,

The problem for Christians— to restate the broader issue once more— is not that their faith is weak or inadequate. In contemporary America, Christians have faith in God and, by and large, they believe and hold fast to the central truths of the Christian tradition. But while they have faith, they have also been formed by the larger post-Christian culture, a culture whose habits of life less and less resemble anything like the vision of human flourishing provided by the life of Christ and witness of scripture. The problem, in other words, is that Christians have not been formed "in all wisdom" that they might rise to the demands of faithfulness in a time such as ours, "bearing fruit in every good work."[73]

So perhaps it is not the Christian church which will lead the nation out of the war against the unborn, or perhaps as they should be called, the people in the womb. Perhaps it is the realization that embracing relativism leads to a bankrupt existence and an empty morality. Perhaps this is what is driving the younger generations as they seek to determine how to best live the lives they have before themselves. It should be noted that despite the increased secularization which is occurring in America, there has been a rising trend in younger people to adopt positions opposing abortion over the last two decades. Surveys are showing that the younger generations tend to be against abortion in far higher percentages than the older generations despite the decline in Christianity. Furthermore, it is more likely for people to move from a pro-choice to a pro-life position than it is to see people moving away from a pro-life stance.

Observationally, there has been a decline in the number of abortions performed each year in the United States as the total number of abortions has gone from 1.6 million per year shortly after *Roe* to 1.3 million a year at the present time.[74] Thus, the sentiment regarding abortion is changing. The question is will it change enough so that all people receive, including those in the womb, the protections that only some people enjoy right now? Even though the younger generations are beginning to accept abortion less than prior generations, there still is no rational basis for this. For the relativistic subjectivism which also is being embraced would suggest that this trend is merely a temporal preference. Ultimately to move towards what is moral, a moral standard must be found. Mark Hanna argues that this is found only in biblical Christianity when he says,

> *Although the philosophical tradition from the time of Socrates often paid lip-service to the values of tolerance and rational discourse, it rarely recognized the intrinsic dignity and equality of all human beings. It was biblical Christianity alone that provided both a sound basis and compelling motivation for universal conformity to these norms. Fundamental to it is the equal dignity of all human beings, which is entailed by the biblical teaching that every person is a bearer of the image of God (Gen. 1:26, 27), that the Son of God was incarnated as a human being (Jn. 1:1, 14), and that Christ died to provide forgiveness and eternal life to all who would trust him (Jn. 12:32; Rom. 10:11-13), and that every person has, as part of the imago Dei, rationality, freedom, and the responsibility to choose truth over falsehood, virtue over vice, and faith in Christ over unbelief (Jn. 7:17).[75]*

Chapter Three

The Abortion Debate

Having examined the historical developments pertaining to abortion it is now time to examine the common arguments which have been used to support abortion. The debate over legalized abortion has been raging for over four decades having intensified since the Supreme Court ruled in Roe which legalized abortion on demand in the United States.

Rather than review the numerous arguments in detail, a general approach will be taken examining the basic categories under which arguments for abortion can be classified. The first category will address the concept of when human life begins from a scientific perspective. Secondly, the concept of personhood will be addressed. Lastly, the various arguments espoused for abortion will be examined.

Biological Science and Humanness

Some have argued that science has not been able to determine when human life begins. However, this argument seems to hold little merit. Humans, just like other living organisms, are viewed by science as coming into existence when they begin to self-replicate and move towards full maturation. This point of coming into existence is almost unanimously determined to be at the point of conception for all mammals including human beings. "All these embryologists and developmental biologists, who are collectively responsible for the standard textbooks in their fields, agree in marking fertilization, not gastrulation, as the beginning of a human individual."[1]

Thus despite what some may argue, the scientific community has for decades determined that human life begins at conception. Attempting to argue that a fertilized egg or zygote is not human does not hold scientific merit, and thus if viewed rationally should be rejected. Once this is established then the natural conclusion is that although human embryos are early in the overall developmental process, they are, "from the very beginning, human beings, sharing an identity with, though younger than, the older human beings they will grow up to become."[2]

Now science does not render moral judgments. Rather science merely establishes what the early zygote is, namely a human being in her earliest stage of development. This being the case, it becomes important to determine philosophically what is deemed to be moral regarding the treatment of human beings. If it is deemed moral to destroy human life, then abortion would certainly fall within the scope of moral conduct. However, if it is deemed immoral to destroy human life in nearly all instances, then this would likewise apply to those individuals in the earliest stages of their development.

Once a moral standard is acknowledged, it in turn will have numerous implications, especially in the scientific realm. If it is immoral to kill a human being for convenience or for the benefit of another, then it is likewise immoral to treat the unborn human beings in this way. The result of remaining consistent with this line of reasoning is that scientific experimentation on human beings, which results in injury or death, should not be permitted regardless of the age of the individual involved. Hence, "the practice of creating and freezing extra embryos as part of IVF should give us serious moral pause. At the very least, this practice should come to an end if we wish to be a culture that treasures life and children and not one that commodifies, instrumentalizes, and mechanizes them."[3]

Even former President Reagan weighed in on the abortion debate when he suggested that the real issue in the abortion debate is not when life begins, which has been scientifically established, but rather the value of human life.[4] Reagan opines that the real problem is that human life in general is not valued sufficiently. He provides the story of Baby Doe as case in point. Baby Doe, who was a child with Down syndrome, was allowed to be starved to death as it was felt that individuals with genetic abnormalities were not of equal value to those without such differences. Hence, Reagan believes that it will not be until human life in general, encompassing all human beings, is valued and protected, that abortion will come to be seen for what it is, an attack on human beings in general.[5]

Personhood in General

The evidence is overwhelming that from the moment of conception, a human being has come in to existence. The debate continues, however, as to when this human being actually attains the status of a person. The concept of personhood as being separate from biological humanity appears to have grown out of the legal language used in the cases which legalized abortion in the United States. The legal reasoning was founded on the concept that a person is protected under the law, but a human being is not. Thus, it was determined that to attain personhood and the associated legal protections and recognition, a human being must actually be born. Since the two rulings establishing abortion on demand throughout the entire time of pregnancy, *Roe v. Wade* and *Doe v. Bolton*, the Court has begun to retract their original conclusion. Today's Supreme Court has begun to view personhood as coming into existence when a baby is able to live independent from its mother, or the age of viability as it is often called. As was previously discussed, with advancing medical technology, the age of viability will continue to fall, perhaps all the way to conception at some future point in time. Hence, the question remains whether the age of establishing personhood likewise will continue to track the age of viability.

The concept of personhood is critical. Are human beings inherently persons or is personhood something that must be attained? Roger Shinn comments on this when he says that,

> *...the case for freedom of abortion and the case against abortion — involve a metaphysical judgment about what it means to be a person. We might prefer not to build law*

on perennially debatable metaphysical judgments. Yet it is hard to detach morality from metaphysics. The reasons why we think it morally different to eat steers than to eat human beings are metaphysical reasons.[6]

D. Scott Henderson further discusses how the metaphysical conclusions about humanity drive the treatment of people in general when he says,

Exactly how one thinks about what constitutes being human in general and being a person in particular directly translates into how one formulates positions on issues such as abortion, embryonic stem cell research, and defining death. Indeed, many of the issues currently under discussion among bioethicists today hinge on the underlying metaphysical assumptions regarding the constitution of human persons.[7]

Norman Geisler also espouses a metaphysical conceptualization of the entire abortion debate as being focused upon the personhood of the unborn. If the unborn is viewed as being fully human then the logical conclusion is that abortion is never acceptable other than in self-defense where the life of the mother is imminently at risk. However, if the unborn is viewed as being subhuman then abortion at any time becomes acceptable.[8] Geisler like many others, appears to premise this position on the basis that it is immoral to take human life in situations other than self-defense. However, as will be discussed shortly, this is not necessarily a shared premise among the members of society in this day and age.

Oddly, over the last four decades there has been a tremendous push in the United States to protect human rights. But what are human rights exactly and what significance do human rights have to this discussion? George and Tollefsen discuss how human rights can be thought of as the very principles that govern how we ought to act or refrain from acting towards other people. Human rights trump our desires when our desires begin to impact and impinge upon the legitimate interests of those who may be affected by what we do.[9]

So what makes a human being human? What is it that separates a human being from all the other animals found on the planet? The one differentiating characteristic that humans possess unlike all the other living creatures on the planet is conceptual thought, the ability to reason, plan, and create. Lee and George further elaborate on this concept.

> *Note that if the analysis just given is substantially correct, then the power of conceptual thought is not just different in degree from other capacities (such as perceptual thought and instinct) but is different in kind. This means that a being either has this capacity or not, even though – as we will indicate more fully later – a being may have a basic natural capacity for conceptual thought long before he or she develops that capacity to the point where it is immediately exercisable (so an infant, for example, has the basic natural capacity for conceptual thought even though it will be months before he or she actually has a concept). Thus, every human being, including human infants and unborn human beings, has this natural capacity for conceptual thought, but a horse or a dog simply and altogether lacks this capacity.[10]*

> *In sum, human beings constitute a special sort of animal. They differ in kind from other animals because they have a rational nature, a nature characterized by having the basic, natural capacities (possessed by each and every human being from the point at which he or she comes to be) for conceptual thought and deliberation and free choice. In virtue of having such a nature, all human beings are persons; and all persons possess the real dignity that is deserving of full moral respect. Thus, every human being deserves full moral respect.[11]*

Having established that human beings are unique among the creatures of the earth, it still does not resolve the problem of when personhood manifests. Or as stated differently, at what point in a human being's development do they become a person. One position is that personhood does not manifest until the human organism is able to demonstrate a variety of characteristics. Some of these are consciousness, the ability to reason, self-motivated activity, the capacity to communicate, and the presence of self-awareness. This approach attempts to define personhood as being related to developmental age and capacities. However, it fails to include all the individuals that we would in a common sense way define as possessing personhood, such as those in comas or those with genetic disorders, Hence when an attempt is made to separate personhood from being human the situation is created where an arbitrary standard is created to define who qualify as persons deserving of protection from society.[12]

An example of where this approach can lead is illustrated by Joseph Fletcher, a situational ethicist. Fletcher takes the argument about characteristics as defining personhood and provides a concrete example. He states that anyone with an IQ of less than twenty on the Stanford-Binet intelligence scale would not qualify as a person and that anyone under forty would be questionable as a person. Fletcher concludes that "if an ape had the intelligence of a human being and the human being had only the capabilities of an ape" that the ape would possess personhood while the human would not. This is the logical outcome of utilizing capabilities and levels of development to define personhood rather than biological humanness.[13] Philosophers have made the distinction between what a human being is in terms of their very essence or humanness and what a human being possesses in terms of characteristics, or as the philosophers say, accidents. The accidents of being human are things such as how tall a person is, what color one's skin is, or even how old he is. Making the distinction between essence and accidents is critical, as the accidents of being human have nothing to do with the essence of humanity. One example of this is that having two arms is an accident of being human. It is easily demonstrated that accidents do not have anything to do with the essence of humanity, as a man who loses an arm in an accident or a child born without arms is still understood as a human being, a possessor of humanness. When making this distinction between accidents and essence the result is that humanness is understood as the very substance of what a person possesses. Hence all humans are persons. "According to the substance view, a human being is intrinsically valuable because of the sort of thing it is and the human being remains that sort of thing as long as it exists."[14]

Further confirmation that the accident/essence distinction is logically sound can be found in the commonly used acronym SLED, developed by Stephen Schwarz, which has become popular when discussing the concept of personhood.[15] This acronym stands for size, level of development, environment, and degree of dependency. It will be demonstrated that these four factors are often used to justify abortion, yet upon examination are irrelevant in determining personhood of a human being.

SLED – Size

The first letter stands for size. Often the size of the unborn is used to justify the lack of possible personhood. It is said that it is not possible to possess personhood when a being is so small. However, when examining the concept of size in isolation it is certainly not the case that smaller adults are entitled to fewer rights than larger adults. Part of what defines a civilized society is that size does not alter a person's ability to access rights which are available to others. All people in society are afforded equal rights. Rights do not accrue based on increases in body mass. Hence, size and or weight do not change the value of a human being.

SLED – Level of Development

The next letter in the acronym stands for the level of development. It has been said that, "Where they disagree is over the question of the moral status of the unborn. These abortion advocates argue that the unborn entity is not a *person* and hence not a subject of moral rights until some decisive moment in fetal or postnatal development."[16] The argument that personhood cannot be bestowed until a certain stage of development is achieved is not consistent with logic or common sense. As previously discussed human beings are biologically human from fertilization onward. Throughout the entire lifespan of a human being, additional abilities can be acquired. Certainly the first twenty-five years contain the most radical new acquisitions of abilities but even in the first seven decades of life and beyond new abilities can be learned. This illustrates that the human being is ever growing and changing over the course of the entire lifespan. As such, setting an arbitrary point in the human's development to claim that personhood has manifested is not sound reasoning. Rushworth Kidder gives an illuminating example which he uses to argue against those who would say that life does not begin at conception. This same argument is applicable to those who would desire to separate personhood from the moment of conception as well.

> He imagines having a large glass urn full of marbles—so many marbles that anyone looking at it would say, "My gosh, that's a lot of marbles!" Suppose you begin removing the marbles, one by one, until there are so few marbles left that anyone looking on would say, "Goodness, there are hardly any marbles in there." Question: Which marble was it that, when you took it out, caused the onlookers to shift from a state of saying "a lot of marbles" to a state of saying "hardly any marbles"? "Obviously, there was no single marble," says Hooker. In that regard, he explains, fetuses are like urns of marbles. "There is no point in the life of a developing human being when you can say, 'Yes, at that point it becomes a human being.' There is no discrete event.... There is no 'moment of conception.' It is a continuum of biochemical events. The concept that there is a moment of conception is unintelligible. It cannot be made real when you reduce it to the level of molecular biology." His point: Only if you can tell me which marble made the difference can I tell you when life begins.[17]

Kidder's example should make it obvious that those who argue that abortion should be permissible prior to viability, or the time the child can live independently from the mother, are merely setting an arbitrary guide. This arbitrary line in the developmental course is an attempt to remove human worth until the line is crossed. However, this fails to acknowledge that the unborn child is human even prior to the current age of viability. As previously stated, as medical technology changes, the age of viability will change and perhaps move back all the way to conception. Thus the age of viability is merely a subjective standard and not suitable for making a moral decision. Lastly, the ability to survive on one's own, or viability, could be applied to adults who live in environments where they could not survive on their own without intervention. Living in extremely cold climates or traveling in space where there is no oxygen are both examples of how relying on external supports to live does not alter one's personhood or humanity.[18]

This also applies to a human being's level of consciousness. Some argue that a baby is not human until it possess self-consciousness. This is used as justification to abort babies in the womb when full consciousness has not yet developed. However, if this were the case then young infants and people in comas could be killed for lacking humanness as well. This same reasoning is applied when arguing that it is acceptable to abort a child before he develops the ability to perceive pain.[19] Again, the ability to experience pain does not define human personhood. If this were the case then those people born with the inability to feel pain would not be seen as human. Obviously this is not the case.

SLED - Environment

The third letter stands for environment. Some have attempted to argue that the particular environment is relevant in determining personhood and human value. However, birth does not change the status of an individual, it only changes his location. Thus arguing that it is acceptable to treat the unborn in one manner and the born in a different manner does not make sense.[20] It merely becomes a statement of environmental discrimination. This asserts that those individuals currently in the womb lack value, yet individuals who have moved to a location outside of the womb now have somehow come to possess human value. This line of reasoning fails as it assigns greater value to an eight month old who lives outside of the womb than to a same aged peer who currently resides in the womb.

Although logically fallacious, legally this seems to be the case. It is lawful to end the life of a child at eight months of age in many states if the mother decides that it is best for her health. However, it is unlawful in all fifty states to end the life of a child who has been born prematurely at eight months of age even when a mother believes that caring for the newly born eight month old would be detrimental to her health and well-being. Once a child is born the law's protections change. Again this was discussed as an artifact of the Supreme Court's rulings in which the Court tried to justify why abortion would be acceptable.

In fact, most abortions occur in the first trimester because the pregnant woman does not desire to have the child. But if the law does not allow a woman to choose to end the life of her child once the child is born, why does the law allow the discriminatory act of allowing such a decision to be applied merely because the child resides in the mother's womb? "If it is unjust to kill a three-year-old child or a three-day-old child because he or she is undesired, then it is likewise unjust to kill a living human before birth. The bottom line is that undesirability is not a just moral basis to kill a human being."[21]

SLED – Degree of Dependency

The last letter stands for the degree of physical dependency. This argument seems to have been incorporated into the Supreme Court's commentary regarding the age of viability. It is often argued that before a child can live independently that the child is not fully human. However, many people who have attained adulthood are not able to live independently and are therefore dependent on others to survive. Is dependency in the young and old truly so different?

Although some would argue that the mother has a right to her own body and that the child is a mere extension possessing none of its own rights, this argument fails on biological grounds. Although the child is dependent, the child is a unique human being who has a unique set of DNA, his own blood type, and his own brain waves. The baby merely is receiving nourishment from the mother which eventually he will receive from other sources when he leaves the mother's womb.[22]

This is akin to the many adults who rely on others to feed them or on medical devices to breathe for them so that they can sustain life. Without the assistance of others or other devices, these dependent people would die. Yet, it is not often said that these dependent people have no right to have their lives protected. It can therefore be concluded that the degree of dependency an individual manifests does not change the individual's human status or their human value.

Arguments for Abortion

For I am impressed that in spite of the hundreds of articles published defending or opposed to abortion, the way people decide to have or not to have an abortion rarely seems to involve the issues discussed in those articles. People contemplating abortion do not ask if the fetus has a right to life, or when does life begin, or even if abortion is right or wrong.[23]

After reviewing the multitude of arguments both for and against abortion some authors have concluded that neither the pro-choice or pro-life groups utilize effective argumentation. One such author is Bernard Nathanson. He believes the anti-abortionists use too many specious arguments. Claiming that the abortion doctors are just greedy physicians with no concern for life or that allowing abortion will lead to the approved killing of other members of society, to Dr. Nathanson, are arguments based in peripheral issues and emotionalism. In line with this assessment, Dr. Nathanson also criticizes the anti-abortionists for using graphic pictures and descriptions of the abortion process to bring about an emotional reaction from the public to persuade them.

On the other side of the debate are those endorsing a pro-choice position whom Nathanson labels as the pro-abortionists. He also criticizes their arguments as faulty. Nathanson provides an example of one such fallacious argument which is used that claims that without abortion there would be overpopulation in the world. Two other false arguments identified by Nathanson are that the unborn child is just mere tissue like an appendage and secondly, that the choice to utilize abortion is only the woman's to make as she should have complete control over her own body. Furthermore, Nathanson refutes perhaps the most common argument used by pro-abortionists when he states that the fear of having to return to illegal back alley abortions which are performed with a coat hanger is pure myth. Nathanson describes how the technology contained in the suction curette developed in 1970 and the available prostaglandin suppositories that will induce a woman to miscarry remove the need for any woman to be subject to a coat hanger abortion even if abortion were made illegal.[24]

Nathanson, although critical of both sides in the abortion debate, concludes that rather than engage in hyperbole, peripheral distractions, and emotionalism, people should focus on the nature of what is developing in the womb and how it should be valued and protected. Interestingly, Nathanson does not take a firm stand on the issue of abortion himself.[25]

In light of Nathanson's criticism, the common arguments utilized to justify the need for abortion will be addressed below. People in favor of abortion tend to espouse arguments that focus on one of three factors: the self, the other, and the world. By grouping the various arguments utilizing this typology it will allow the general concepts conveyed in each argument to be addressed.

Arguments Focused on the Self

A Woman's Rights

At the core of the arguments focused on the self are the concepts of a woman's rights. These rights span the right to privacy, the right to exercise choice, and the right to exert bodily control. Often these rights are discussed as if they were absolute rights possessed by women in the United States. However, as R. C. Sproul says, "The right to control one's own body is not an absolute right."[26] Sproul argues that the right to privacy and the right to exercise choice regarding one's body and life are transcended by the right to life.

The argument that the right to life supersedes all other rights does possess merit. The conflict of rights does seem to be at the very heart of the abortion debate. Who has rights and whose rights are more important become key questions when trying to draw proper conclusions amidst the often emotionally charged arguments embraced by participants in this debate.

George and Tollefsen discuss the concept of rights and offer their suggested method of resolving the conflict between the right to privacy and the right to life.

> *First—and this is true of abortion as well—it is difficult to see how any form of killing of human beings could properly be considered a private matter. By the nature of the case, two individuals are involved; moreover, in this particular type of case, one of the individuals does not consent. Most important, killing is essentially a violation of the most basic form of community available to human beings, a community that is prepolitical but inescapably "public".*[27]

> *We argued that the right to life, unlike the right to vote, does not vary from place to place or time to time for the same entity. This is because the right to life is in a strong and obvious sense the foundational right for persons. It is the right upon which all other rights are predicated and marks whether a being is a being of moral standing at all. If the right to life depended upon, for example, a particular and exercisable ability, then some human beings would possess that right earlier than others, and some would never possess it.*[28]

Therefore the right to choose an abortion for a woman removes the right to choose life for the unborn child. It is fair to ask what makes a woman's right to choose more important than the unborn's right to choose or the unborn's right to life for that matter? Other authors have further added the concept that a parent has a duty to her unborn child which is based in the concept of community. In essence, no one exists in isolation, and therefore others' rights must be entertained when we as individuals desire to exercise our own rights. As a result, parents must entertain the rights of their children, which therefore imposes a duty on parents to seek to protect and care for their children as members of the larger community in which all people are participants. Thus, the exercise of living out such duty is morally required and will likely bring each of us some discomfort and pain as our personal desires often are usurped by the needs of others to which we owe this communal duty.[29]

However, when comparing the imposition created by the duty to tend to and care for another, inconvenience still does not trump the right to life.

> *The burdens of pregnancy include physical difficulties and the pain of labor, and can include significant financial costs, psychological burdens, and interference with autonomy and the pursuit of other important goals. These costs are not inconsiderable. Partly for that reason we owe our mothers gratitude for carrying and giving birth to us. However, where pregnancy does not place a woman's life in jeopardy or threaten grave and lasting damage to her physical health, the harm done to other goods is not total. Moreover, most of the harms involved in pregnancy are not irreversible: pregnancy is a nine-month task – if the woman and man are not in a good position to raise the child, adoption is a possibility. So the difficulties of pregnancy, considered together, are in a different and lesser category than death. Death is not just worse in degree than the difficulties involved in pregnancy; it is worse in kind....the burden of carrying the baby, for all its distinctness, is significantly less than*

the harm the baby would suffer by being killed; the mother
and father have a special responsibility to the child; it
follows that intentional abortion (even in the few cases
where the baby's death is an unintended but foreseen side
effect) is unjust and therefore objectively immoral.[30]

Elizabeth Fox-Genovese makes an important observation regarding this conflict of rights which arises in the case of pregnancy. "Our challenge is to turn the clock forward by offering women new visions that do not put their lives against the lives of their children in a Darwinian struggle for survival. In that struggle, no one wins."[31]

Women's Safety

The next set of arguments for abortion are primarily focused on self-concern and suggest that a woman's safety is a paramount reason to allow for abortion to be performed. Unfortunately, the definition of health when broadened can become far more expansive than what many people might initially assume. Bosgra describes the problem succinctly when he says, "When abortion is considered acceptable to preserve the health of the mother, it opens up the door for widespread abuse. Suddenly the health of the mother can be construed as inconvenience or mental stress or mere physical difficulty such as exhaustion rather than any true life threatening situation."[32]

Bosgra supports his contention with the finding that in states where abortion was first legalized for the protection of a mother's health, that mental health reasons were being used to justify abortions. Hence any woman who felt emotionally distressed as a result of the pregnancy suddenly had a justifiable reason to terminate the life of her child. It is often argued that women who feel overwhelmed with pregnancy may as a result become suicidal. However, numerous physicians and psychiatrists have stated that this claim is a fallacy which does not stand up to statistical or clinical scrutiny.[33]

Therefore it is germane to the debate to note that the incidence of pregnancy where a mother's life is truly threatened by the pregnancy is very low. In these rare circumstances where a mother's life is truly threatened, such as in a tubal pregnancy, it must be noted that the pregnancy will not be able to develop sufficiently for the child to survive even with currently available medical intervention. These circumstances will result in the death of the child at a minimum, and without intervention, the death of the mother as well. Hence, intervening to save the mother's life attempts to preserve life to the greatest extent possible. However, it must be remembered that circumstances such as these are extremely rare given the advances in medical technology that allow for supporting a child that may need to be delivered prior to full term.

Others have argued that being forced to have a child and then possibly giving that child up for adoption, results in such psychological trauma that abortion is necessary to protect the mother's emotional health. Although it is true that a woman may experience regret and sadness about having to give a child up for adoption, it is hard to imagine how placing a child in an adoptive setting is more emotionally traumatizing than knowing the child was killed. Perhaps an abortion seems like a quick fix in the moment, but there is no undoing the act once it has occurred. An adopted child, in most circumstances, can still have contact with his or her parents during the child's life if such contact is desired. Additionally, the claim that giving a child up for adoption is more traumatizing than having an abortion is not supported by the research that has been done. Despite the lack of empirical evidence, some authors still attempt to utilize the potential trauma of placing a child in an adoptive setting as a reason for maintaining readily available abortion access, thus arguing that abortion protects the health of women.[34]

In terms of physical health, claiming that abortion safeguards the health of women becomes even less compelling. Dr. Shadigian cites the research findings which indicate that women are actually at greater risk physically for a number of disorders if they have an abortion.

"Nonetheless, given a few methodological caveats, current research suggests that a history of induced abortion is associated with an increased long-term risk of: 1) breast cancer; 2) placenta previa; 3) pre-term birth; 4) maternal suicide."[35] Dr. Shadigian also comments on how women who have abortions are actually at a higher overall risk of death in the year following the abortion than the general public.[36] As such, the empirical research does not support that abortion is necessary for protecting women's health, but in fact finds just the opposite: abortion is a danger to women's health both physical and mental.

Concluding this section, it is time to address the predominant argument pertaining to women's health. It has been argued repeatedly that without legal abortion that thousands of women would die each year from illegal abortions. However, the belief that thousands of women died from illegal abortions prior to abortion being legalized was created by false statements made by Dr. Bernard Nathanson. In Dr. Nathanson's book he admits that he knowingly cited false statistics as it was his desire to get abortion legalized. Dr. Nathanson stated that the Federal government reported only one hundred sixty deaths from abortion in 1967 and only thirty-nine deaths in 1972.[37] The truth is that without legalized abortion, women's safety is in no greater jeopardy. Additionally, the fact that there are 1.5 million children who are aborted in the United States alone, means that without legal abortion the unborn women and men will be far safer as there will be over a million fewer deaths each year.[38]

Pregnancy is Incompatible with Career & Education

Another primary argument for justifying abortion rests in the concept that for women to be happy and to exercise the freedoms afforded to individuals in today's workplace, readily available abortion is necessary for women. The empirical research has demonstrated consistently that the most common argument offered for having an abortion is that continuing the pregnancy will jeopardize one's future.[39]

Although many have been convinced by this argument, it actually undermines the very nature of womanhood which involves bearing children. How can a woman's future be put at risk when she is performing the very thing that her body was created to do? The answer can be found in how society has adopted the perspective that women can be equal to men in every way. Hence, women must somehow dispose of part of their biological functioning if they are to be perceived as true equals in this day and age. Elizabeth Fox-Genovese describes how those supporting abortion have used the current push for equality and the impact it has on women. "The simple answer lies in their success in convincing people that full personhood for women depends upon being truly equal to men – which effectively means securing freedom from their bodies and, especially, from children."[40] Thus a woman cannot experience full womanhood if she hopes to be considered equal to men in today's society.

The grave danger in the current sociological climate for women is that it appears that women who are independent and not conflicted about choosing to abort their child because they see their pregnancy as interfering with their career, education, or financial situation are practically speaking, living out the historically male persona. These women are often cited in the research as being satisfied with their choice to abort their children in an effort to maintain their desired career and educational goals. This is destructive to the sense of inherent worth in womanhood.

On the other hand, women who have adopted the historical feminine identity, who perceive themselves as mothers and tend to be dependent upon others financially, have been reported in the research to struggle with making a decision to abort their child. This conflict leads to increased suffering and more negative effects for the woman if she indeed does abort her child. What this suggests is that women who adhere to a historical and biblical view or identity of womanhood tend to have a much harder time choosing to abort their children and suffer significantly more if they do abort their children.

Those women who have adopted a male identity in an attempt to fit into the modern work world and culture tend to perceive their pregnancy as a threat to what they desire for themselves. As such, aborting their child does not lead to apparent distress to the same extent, rather it turns into a situation where it's either the child or the woman which will survive. As has been previously discussed, the battle between the mother and unborn child leaves the child in the losing position in all circumstances, as the child cannot speak for herself and does not possess the power to assert her position in desiring life against the mother's contrary position. The competitive mindset has worked historically for men who struggle to climb the corporate ladder and in the process often have to compete with other people where weakness is seen as a deficit and strength and victory over another person is seen as an asset and is rewarded. The unfortunate circumstance for women however, is when this mode of operation plays out between a woman and her child, the child who is the weaker party, will nearly always lose. Unlike men where the loss may result in a failure to be promoted, the loss for a woman and her child means the loss of the child's life.[41]

This self-focused argument that abortion is necessary for women to be able to live out the work and educational lives they desire has far larger implications for society. Ultimately society must support women in their biological role of carrying and raising children if women, who are now often expected to single handedly raise their children, are to conceivably balance the roles of motherhood and bread winner.

Rape & Incest

The last argument for abortion focused primarily on the self is also the most emotionally charged. This is the argument that a woman who conceives after being a victim of rape or incest should be entitled to an abortion. This argument is premised in the belief that a woman who does not choose to become pregnant, should not be forced to carry a child. In essence, a woman who has not consented to a pregnancy has no binding duty to continue a pregnancy.

First of all, in cases of rape, it is very rare that a pregnancy results. It has been reported to occur less than one percent of the time. Additionally, if a woman seeks immediate treatment after a rape, pregnancy can be prevented in all cases with the current medical treatments that are available. Pregnancy resulting from rape is therefore rare and certainly an exceptional situation. To argue that abortion needs to be available because of the small minority of women who become pregnant each year resulting from rape holds little merit. It is a hasty generalization and a logical fallacy. Furthermore, even when women do become pregnant after a rape it is observed that about half of the women want to keep the child. For the other fifty percent of women, adoption is always an option.[42]

Even among many people who do not support abortion in general, they make an exception for pregnancies that result from a rape. This suggests how entrenched the concept of individual freedom has become in the modern world, as the right to freedom is oftentimes valued above the right to life. It is commonly believed that to force a woman to have a child conceived from rape is to only further the trauma to the woman. But it must be understood that when a woman is raped and conceives a child the baby becomes a co-victim with the mother. To kill the unborn baby would be committing another heinous crime and add the evil of murder to the evil of rape.[43] Punishing the unborn child does not remove the crime that was committed against the mother and hence adoption is by far the better option when compared with abortion.[44]

Beckwith illustrates this with an example based in comparing a situation where a man has his sperm stolen by an unscrupulous person who then inseminates a woman with the sperm. When the child that is born, being his biological offspring, is now by court order granted monthly support from the man whose sperm was stolen. This would cause great emotional and financial difficulty for him and yet would it be right for him to kill the child to end the injustice which had been done to him? He did not consent to the child's birth and yet by law is now bound to provide for this child. This is the analogous situation to a woman who was raped who has had a great injustice done to her and the subsequent pregnancy would lead to financial and emotional difficulty as well. Neither the man in the illustration or the woman who was raped have a moral obligation to raise the child, but this still does not allow for either of them to kill the human being who was conceived due to the injustice against either of them "… It seems that the more general obligation not to directly kill another human person does apply to both the sperm donor and the rape victim."[45]

Arguments Focused on the Other – The Unborn Child

Prior to Birth a Child is Not a Full Member of Society

The next set of arguments for abortion are premised on making determinations about what is in the unborn child's best interest, as well as when the unborn child actually comes to have any recognition societally. This ties in again with the concept of when personhood is bestowed upon a person. If a human being does not receive recognition of personhood at conception and thus is not viewed as possessing the full rights and protections of other people in society then the question is at what point does this occur?

Many have made arbitrary distinctions in an effort to separate human life from human personhood. "Making a pseudoscientific discrimination between two 'kinds' of life, or two 'kinds' of human beings, merely smuggles in moral considerations under the guise of scientific respectability."[46]

In the past those in favor of abortion tried to distinguish when human life begins. However, the focus has now switched from when human life begins to when a human life comes to possess personhood. As Fowler states, "The main spokespersons for abortion are no longer trying to deny the humanity of the unborn. Virtually all agree that 'human life' begins at conception… Instead they are making a new and crucial distinction between human life and a human being — that is, between biological life and personhood." Now those in favor of abortion are saying it is improper to use the terms human life and person interchangeably as they view personhood as something that develops after human life begins.[47] Only by separating personhood from human life can those favoring abortion continue to rationalize abortion as acceptable.

If the unborn child is not a full-fledged member of the human community then there would be no real duty to offer protection to the unborn. However, if the unborn is a human being and a full member of the community, then the various arguments which cite career impairments, rape, genetic abnormality, or an unwanted child fail to be persuasive. More so, they become morally reprehensible.[48]

Avoiding Unwanted Children and Preventing Their Future Abuse

More recently those favoring abortion argue that by allowing children to be aborted that it prevents their future abuse by parents not interested in raising these children. It is argued that if children who are not wanted are born that they will be subject to being abused and neglected. However, the research does not demonstrate this to be the case and killing a child is certainly the worst form of abuse that exists.[49]

In fact research studies have found this argument to be without merit. "Physical child abuse is rarely related to an unwanted pregnancy." Child abuse statistics from Hawaii, New York, Arizona, and Colorado during the early 1970s indicated an increase in child abuse cases after abortion was legalized, not a decrease. Furthermore Dr. Edward Lenoski, a professor of pediatrics at the University of

Southern California, studied fractures in children under the age of six and found that in his sample of approximately five thousand cases that ninety-two percent of those abused as children were from planned pregnancies. Thus it appears as if there is very little linkage between unwanted pregnancy and child abuse.[50]

Another version of this argument is that no one should be forced to shoulder an unwanted burden. If having a child is an undesired burden then having the child should be optional. With the Supreme Court ruling in *Eisenstadt v. Baird* (1972) which stated that people have the right to have non-procreative sex, pregnancy came to be viewed as an unwanted burden. However, regardless of what the Supreme Court may say, pregnancy is the natural result of the act of sexual intercourse. Hence, the possibility of pregnancy is always present when engaging in sexual intercourse. As such, pregnancy even if perceived as a burden is a natural result of the choices made by the people involved. When a new person is brought into existence his or her rights must also be weighed, and in so doing it becomes apparent that abortion is not an option as it imposes the mother's desire to be free from the burden of pregnancy upon the unborn's right to life. Taken to its logical conclusion, this argument could also be used for ending the life of infants and other children who are viewed as a burden due to their needs for maternal care.[51]

Jean Garton is reported to have made the astute observation that when people make comments about a child as being precious or naughty they are commenting about the child. But when people say a child is unwanted, they are not describing the child but rather describing themselves and revealing the deficiencies they possess. "The unwanted child is not the victim of his own shortcomings but that of his parents."[52] Yet again, the regularity of the argument for abortion based in the concept that people should not have to have children that are not going to be wanted is a reflection upon how society at large has become self-focused to the neglect of others.

Perhaps a stronger appearing argument, but ultimately equally unsound, is the argument that children with physical and genetic abnormalities are better off if they are aborted. The argument takes the position that if a child has abnormalities that he will not be able to experience a quality of life that is worth living. Hence, ending his life early will save the child from future unnecessary suffering and ultimately is in the child's best interest. However, when speaking to those individuals who live with genetic and physical deformities they report experiencing quality lives. So far no group representing the disabled has yet to come out in support of abortion as being desired by those with disabilities.[53]

Elizabeth Schiltz describes how she had a child with Down syndrome. She reflects upon how he would have been sent to a death camp if he had been born in Germany where she grew up. Her anecdote touches on how each human life is significant, on how even people without perfect genetics are still human and deserving of being treated as such.[54]

Being human expresses itself in many ways as every human being is unique. When value judgments are made which restrict full personhood to those people who fit within certain parameters or possess specific characteristics, inevitably many human beings will be excluded from the realm of humanity. When we begin to exclude some of our fellow members of the human community and place them in disenfranchised positions we ultimately undermine our very standing as members in the human community.

> ... *A human being, at every stage of her development is never a potential person; she is always a person with potential even if that potential is never actualized due to premature death or the result of the absence or deformity of a physical state necessary to actualize that potential.*[55]

Arguments Focused on the World

Equality of Women in Society

Lastly, the arguments for abortion which focus on the best interests of the world will be examined. It is often argued that abortion is necessary to maintain social, political, and economic equality between men and women. Again this is premised in the concept that for women to be truly equal to men that they cannot be expected to be responsible for carrying and raising children. However, this line of argumentation is flawed for inherent in this argument is the assumption that men are naturally superior to women. This position holds that women, being naturally inferior to men due to their biology, require an elective surgery known as abortion to maintain equality with men.[56]

When described in this manner the argument sounds laughable, yet the desire for women to be perceived and to function as equal to men has led to this situation where a woman cannot be a woman if she desires equality as equality is now defined. However, this equality is based in biological equivalency. As such, women will never attain equality because they will never be men. Ultimately, "the key to ending this inequality is not to socialize women into the male paradigm, but to celebrate and honor the indispensable role that mothers play in caring for the most vulnerable and defenseless members of our population, the unborn."[57]

Abortion Has Been Determined To Be Legal

Another argument for abortion which is based in cultural and societal influence is the position that states that abortion is acceptable because it is legal. It has been noted that although those opposed to abortion have had some success in restricting access to abortion services, less progress has been made in the legal arena which still is endorsing abortion on demand. Currently abortion is still legal in an unrestricted manner through the fifth month of pregnancy in the United States and much of the developed world. Although many applaud this current legal climate, others have noted that legalized abortion has not represented progress for women and the United States but rather represents a significant decline in the position and value of women.

By trivializing and even denigrating women's ability to bear children, legalized abortion has stripped women of their distinct dignity as women; it has shredded the primary tie among women of different classes, races, ethnicities and national origins; it has seriously diminished women's prospects for marriage and even further diminished their prospects for a lasting marriage; and it has exposed them

to unprecedented levels of sexual exploitation. Welcome to
the brave new world of freedom, ladies – and gentlemen.[58]

Additionally, legalized abortion is premised on the legal concepts of freedom of choice, the right to privacy, and the right to pursue enjoyment without consequences (non-procreative sex). What has consistently been absent from the legal discussion by the Supreme Court are the rights of the unborn. As such, "Justice for the unborn takes a second seat to pity for the mother."[59] Sadly this is not the case when non-humans are dealt with in the legal arena. One notable example is how baby eagles and eagles' eggs are protected under the law along with adult eagles. But this is not the case for those of the human race.[60]

Former President Ronald Reagan suggests that the Supreme Court itself might overturn *Roe v. Wade* just as it had overturned prior decisions that were related to the issue of personhood. "They did it by appealing to the hearts and minds of their countrymen, to the truth of human dignity under God. From their example, we know that respect for the sacred value of human life is too deeply ingrained in the hearts of our people to remain forever suppressed." Reagan refers to the Dred Scott decision of 1857 and how it took a number of decades to ultimately be overturned by a Court that at one point had determined that certain ethnic groups were less human based upon their skin color alone.[61] Although the law may not always be consistent and logical it does not remove the duty that all citizens and human beings have to strive to correct the law when it fails to serve as the equal protector of all people. All human beings, including human beings at the beginning of their lives, have rights that may not be violated and must be protected by law, including the right to life.

Overpopulation

The last argument in this category is the argument that without abortion the world would suffer from overpopulation. Those in favor of abortion argue that without abortion the entire human race would be in jeopardy. They claim that the world could not support the fifty million or so individuals who would be born without abortion being available on a worldwide basis. This is a specious argument as the world is not suffering from a shortage of material resources. Rather, it is the distribution of these resources such as food and water that is problematic. The distribution problems are caused by the greed of those controlling the resources. In the United States farmers are even paid not to grow crops so the crop prices can be manipulated. Regardless of the change in population, this has nothing to do with determining if it is moral to take the life of an unborn child.[62]

Chapter Four

Can The Abortion Debate Be Resolved?

Having reviewed the primary arguments for abortion it is now time to examine why abortion still generates such controversy. From a scientific perspective that takes biology into account or from a philosophical and moral perspective that takes personhood into account it would appear that there is not much left to say regarding abortion. The matter is clear to most who examine it. However, this clarity finds itself manifesting in two ways. There are those that say, "Yes I have examined abortion from the scientific, philosophical, and moral perspectives and you are right, it is perfectly clear that abortion should be freely available." This is the conclusion opposite from what logic would seem to demand. Yet those adhering to the position supporting abortion still thrive in society and the world. So how can the same information lead to contrary conclusions? Has there been an error in reasoning?

This chapter will focus on the concept of worldview and how one's worldview actually shapes the way that information is organized and processed. This author believes that it is the difference in worldview that leads to such contrary conclusions in the abortion debate as well as to the adoption of different ethical systems. This becomes relevant in that one's ethical system guides the understanding of what is right and wrong, what one ought and ought not to do.

Worldviews

And if the pro-choice side could be persuaded that life began at conception, they would have no interest in ending that life, since "choice" does not imply that individuals ought to be allowed to decide whether or not to commit murder. What keeps these sides apart? Not their values, which line up with remarkable congruence. What separates them is their definitions.[1]

A worldview "as Charles Colson has defined it, is 'the sum total of our beliefs about the world, the 'big picture' that directs our daily decisions and actions.... [it] is a way of seeing and comprehending all reality."[2] Thus a person's worldview becomes crucial as it forms his thinking and guides his actions. This can be both positive and negative depending on which worldview is adopted. Ultimately worldviews can be compared, and since they oppose one another they all cannot be correct. Hence, the various worldviews can be compared to determine which is the most likely of being true by evaluating them to determine which worldview best corresponds to reality.

Although the above quote from Kidder suggests that mere definitions keep the pro-choice and pro-life sides apart, the research suggests that it is more than definitions. In fact many women who opt to have an abortion actually believe that they are murdering their babies. Yet, they proceed to do so. Certainly there is no definitional divide that explains this choice for these women. There is something more foundational that drives the decision to do something that people believe is generally wrong even if it is societally acceptable. This can be explained in large part by the observation that people display moral depravity regardless of their worldview.

In fact, people can be quite inconsistent in formulating a worldview and yet the one consistent aspect observed in all people at all times is moral depravity. Hence, moral depravity causes people to act in ways that even they believe are wrong. As opposed to many of the modern philosophers who desire to frame people as being born morally good, actual data suggests that people are born morally depraved and then they work to try and keep this depravity in check over the course of their lives. It is for this very reason that societies require laws as the various laws serve as an additional mechanism to curb immoral conduct.

Given that human moral depravity is observed in all people regardless of the worldview they hold, it can be viewed as a contributing factor in the abortion debate; even though the significance of worldviews is much less relevant in understanding the actual behavior of women seeking abortion. Rather, the significance of worldviews is found in the actual abortion debate itself as the various worldviews held by the constituents of the debate impact the reasoning and conclusions which are espoused.

Although not discussing all the worldviews, the three predominant worldviews held today are theism, pantheism, and atheism. It is interesting that when comparing worldviews the primary differences are tied to their views about God, human beings, and the world. Hence worldviews are comprehensive in scope covering all of what is conceived in our existence.

Beginning with theism, the view of God will be compared. Theism holds that there is a personal God who created the universe but who is not a part of it. This view understands that God is the all-powerful being who brought everything that we know as the universe into being out of nothingness.

Pantheism holds that the entire universe and all things in it are God. This belief says that God is all and all is God. In essence, God is in everything in the universe and the universe as a whole comprises the being of God. Thus, God is the mountain, the stars, the ocean, and of course God exists in every person. Following this belief it is evident that every person is likewise part of God and contains the divine within themselves.

Lastly is the belief that says that the universe is all there is and that there is no God. This view is referred to as atheism which believes that the universe began with a big bang and that all life has evolved to be what it is today. Atheists are often referred to as secular humanists and they generally believe that human beings are the highest form of life that is currently known in the universe.[3] Below is a table which details two worldviews: theism and atheism.

The Theistic Judeo-Christian View and Atheistic Secular Humanist Worldviews:[4]

Judeo-Christian	Secular Humanist
There is a Creator.	*There is no Creator.*
Humankind was specially created.	*Humankind evolved from animals.*
God is sovereign over life.	*Humankind is sovereign over life.*
Sanctity of life is a key principle.	*Quality of life is a key principle.*
The end does not justify the means.	*The ends justify the means.*

The differences in the worldviews listed in the table reveal how people can come to such opposing conclusions about a matter such as abortion. With the theistic worldview God is seen as the one who gives life and thus is the possessor of the authority to decide if life is to be taken. However, in the atheistic worldview human beings are seen as the sovereigns over life and therefore are the ones to determine the circumstances under which life can be taken. When it comes to morality, the theists believe morality comes from the nature of God and is thus absolute. Atheists, on the other hand, view morality as coming from people and as having an evolutionary nature, which means that there is no absolute morality but only consensus that can change over time.

It becomes evident that these two systems clash in the matter of abortion because of their rival premises. The challenge in our society is that we have no agreed upon mechanism for weighing or comparing one premise with another.[5] As such the two sides remain deadlocked with no hope of reaching agreement.

From one perspective, we must choose between life and death; from the other, it is choice versus oppression. When the stakes are so high, compromise is an evasion. These binary oppositions are institutionalized into our legal system. Abortion is legal— or, given a few new Supreme Court judges, it will become illegal. For many, Roe v. Wade represents the stranglehold of "the culture of death." For many others, it is a beacon of freedom and hope for all women.[6]

"Any rational method for resolving moral disagreements requires a shared tradition that embodies assumptions about the nature of man and our true end."[7] Although the United States did possess a shared theistic tradition at one point in time, this no longer is the case. Hence, the current difficulty with resolving matters, such as abortion, in the public square where opposing worldviews compete for supremacy. As people who possess contrary worldviews attempt to reach agreement, ultimately it is not the observable facts which will be the points of contention, but rather the interpretation of the significance of the facts as they pertain to proper moral conduct for all people.

Morality Found in Worldview

It has been stated that research findings tend to be value free. That is, they are descriptive not prescriptive. Thus Pellegrin concludes that when citing research to support a position it must be remembered that the research itself cannot legitimately be used "...to argue for social policies that are dependent on value judgments."[8] When groups like the American Psychological Association (APA) attempt to use empirical research findings to determine what is moral, a logical error in reasoning occurs. Research data which is descriptive does not address that which is prescriptive. Pellegrin attempts to remain neutral in the matter of determining morality by allowing philosophers to address the domain of morality while limiting the extent to which empirical findings are utilized.

Pellegrin then argues that the APA's position on abortion is an error where the APA improperly moves from empirical observations to moral prescriptives. Just because psychologists have determined that there are no adverse psychological consequences to the act of having an abortion, does not indicate that the APA should endorse a pro-choice position. This is the leap from is to ought that is logically fallacious. Rather, Pellegrin argues that the proper position of psychology is to provide behavioral evidence related to the consequences of competing social policies but not to take a stand for either side.[9]

However, in the realm of morality it has been discussed that there are two opposing sides. The theists that hold to an absolute set of moral standards and the atheists who hold that moral standards are relative. Although not completely consistent, theists tend to oppose abortion as a violation of God's moral law while atheists, as well as pantheists, tend to be supportive of abortion for those who desire it. "… Many of us are afraid to speak our truth." Runkle is one such author who takes the position that there is no absolute truth, but rather each person has to define their own truth.[10]

Claire is yet another author who similarly holds to this position when she says that her research has convinced her that there is no such thing as a universal or absolute morality which is applicable to all people at all times.[11] Holding this view, Claire states that the problem with religious groups who assist women who have had abortions is that they etch their religious beliefs into their teachings. Claire does not believe abortion to be a religious or moral issue per se but rather the choice that all women should be able to make to suit themselves.[12] Again, this is consistent with her worldview. She concludes that if you have reached a conclusion that abortion is morally wrong that you have formed an opinion deserving of respect, but no more respect than if you reached a conclusion that abortion was morally proper. As such she reiterates her view that there is no absolute morality but rather moral standards are to be determined by each individual.[13]

Determining personal moral guidelines is only the beginning when adopting an atheistic or secular humanistic worldview. This personal deterministic model where the self is the supreme decision maker extends to the issue of defining when life begins as well as when a human being will be recognized as possessing personhood. Claire illustrates this point when she says that what "the advocates of adoption as an alternative to abortion fail to realize is that a born baby is NOT the same as an embryo or fetus in utero. A willingness to have an abortion does not mean that a woman would be willing to give up a baby."[14] Claire tries to make the distinction between a baby that is in the uterus and a baby that is no longer in the uterus. However, this is merely a matter of location and has nothing to do with the nature of the baby as has been discussed in the prior chapter.

Moving from self-determined morality to the nature and character of God further illustrates the differences between the worldviews. Runkle who adopts a position fairly consistent with pantheism provides guidance for those women who may be contemplating having an abortion.

> *Getting your answers on paper is like making a map of your own conscience. This map can reveal the inner wisdom that is already part of you. And the writing process itself can be a form of prayer, asking for guidance from a Power greater than yourself, so that you will come to know in your heart what is the right decision....Does this mean God? Yes – the God of your understanding.*[15]

Again Runkle makes it clear that she believes that each person is the determiner of truth, and as such she can create a God of her own choosing, which in essence makes her God. She assumes as much by saying that the wisdom of God is already within each person.

Others who subscribe to the humanistic worldview conclude that it really does not matter what a pregnant woman does as long as she chooses to do something that is consistent with her moral outlook. In essence, the significant factor to be considered is that the woman makes decisions autonomously and in concert with her own self-determined sense of right and wrong.[16]

This can only be possible if the self is the originator of the moral standard, which in turn reduces morality to a personal decision based on one's own experience.

Runkle does summarize the opposing worldview conclusions when she attempts to summarize the positions in the abortion debate by describing those in the pro-choice camp as taking the position that we as people have the right to decide for ourselves what is best, what is true, and what is morally proper. Those in the pro-life camp however, are described as taking the position that it is God that decides what is best, true, and moral. Runkle rightly identifies the critical distinction in dealing with this issue between those holding opposing worldviews.[17]

Ethical Utilitarianism

Suffering pain in order to do what is right is the mark of a virtuous person. Doing what feels good is often easy. It's not so easy to do what is good.[18]

The above quote is meant to illustrate that doing what is morally proper from a theistic worldview may involve sacrifice on the part of the self. However, those adhering to the ethical system known as utilitarianism might make a similar statement. Utilitarianism is the ethical stance that believes that what ought to be done is that which brings about the best outcome or has the greatest utility. There is some variance within this view in terms of which perspective should be adopted to determine which outcome has the greatest utility but generally the perspective adopted is that of the self. Utilitarianism teaches that we do that which is expedient to bring about the end result. Or stated differently, the end justifies the means.

People are said to do what is right if they act in accord with what brings the best outcome to them. Given that people are shaped by their culture and motivated by their surroundings,[19] it should come as no surprise that ethical utilitarianism does not have a set of fixed moral absolutes. Instead, each person must determine what the proper course of action is in each circumstance. Hence, "a treatment of any moral problem is inadequate if it fails to analyze the morality of a given act in a way that represents the concrete experience of the agent who faces a decision with respect to this act."[20]

This subjective utilitarian approach to morality is endorsed by many pro-choice authors. Unfortunately, advocating for a patient centered approach which begins with helping the woman decide what the best option is for her is at the very root of the problem within the abortion debate. It puts the person as the top level authority in the process of decision making rather than God. If God were at the top then the process would be about trying to determine what option is best for God. This in some ways could still be in line with a utilitarian system. However, most utilitarian ethical advocates today remove God from the decisional process and place the person as sovereign over his or her own life. However, with the person in the top level position the decision becomes what is the best option for that person. This best option for the person likely will be in conflict with what God deems best, and additionally to what the unborn child deems best. It truly is this me versus others perspective that leads to the termination of approximately twenty-five percent of all pregnancies by induced abortion.[21]

The impact of the utilitarian ethic that has pervaded our society is observable when examining the rationale that women give for having an abortion. Finer concluded after doing a survey study that,

It is notable that the women in our survey emphasized their conscious examination of the moral aspects of their decisions. Although some described abortion as sinful and wrong, many of those same women, and others, described the indiscriminate bearing of children as a sin, and their abortion as "the right thing" and "a responsible choice."...They saw not having a child as their best (and sometimes only) option.[22]

Finer's study further demonstrates how the utilitarian ethic has been adopted as the standard for determining morality in our culture. Sadly, the utilitarian ethic often leads to decisions which are contrary to those which would be consistent with maintaining a biblical worldview. The fact that approximately eighty percent of women who are having abortions self-identify as Catholic or Protestant further indicates how this utilitarian ethic has permeated the American culture and Christendom in general.[23]

Although consequentialism is broader than utilitarianism they both are similar in many ways. Utilitarianism as a theory came first and was followed by consequentialism which proposed to evaluate actions on the basis of which option will produce the optimal or best consequences. Again, the challenges faced by utilitarianism, such as having no absolute standard to evaluate consequences, applies equally to consequentialism as well. In the abstract the problem with these ethical approaches can be entertained. In the application of these ethical systems the reality of the horrors that have been perpetrated by people against other people come to light.

> *And this brings us to what is perhaps the most crucial point concerning all forms of utilitarianism and consequentialism: within any such ethic, there always will be human beings who are dispensable, who must be sacrificed for the greater good. Utilitarianism fails in a radical way to respect the dignity and rights of individual human beings. For it treats the greater good, a mere aggregate of all the interests or pleasures or preferences of individuals, as the good of supreme worth and value, and it demands that nothing stand in the way of its pursuit. The utilitarian thus cannot believe, except as a convenient fiction, in human rights or in actions that may never be done to people, regardless of the consequences.*[24]

In addition to the impact that utilitarianism has had in promoting abortion as a necessary option, there are additional implications in the field of biomedical research. How human zygotes and embryos are treated and what is deemed to be acceptable research is determined by what is deemed to be moral or proper. As scientists have adopted utilitarianism as their ethical perspective, the possibility of experimenting on the youngest of human beings, those who have just been formed after conception, becomes acceptable as the greater good of societal advance is seen to outweigh the impact upon the individual in question. This same reasoning is applied to the use of utilizing tissue from aborted children in medical experimentation.

> *Utilitarianism and consequentialism have played a critical role in disposing many people toward treating human embryos as mere material for scientific research. But these are deeply flawed theories: As we have shown, they either rely upon a false theory of value or they attempt to weigh, commensurate, and maximize where it*

*is impossible to do so. They certainly should be rejected as the basis for distinguishing the just from the unjust treatment of human beings at any developmental stage…
All human beings, even in the embryonic stage of their lives, are worthy of full moral respect and should not be reduced to the status of disposable research material.*[25]

Theistic Ethical Absolutism

Ethical absolutism is the perspective that states that there are absolute moral standards that do not change. These standards are true for all people at all times and in all places. This ethical perspective is consistent with a theistic worldview as these absolute moral standards are understood to be rooted in the ever constant nature of God. When examining cultures from around the world, it is found that people in all cultures have held to the same basic moral standards such as not committing murder or stealing from others. Since ethical absolutism is rooted in the nature of God, the moral standards can likewise be found in God's revealed will in the Bible. This being the case, the Bible then serves as the revelation of God's moral will for all people.

From the time of the Old Testament, ethics have been viewed as universal for all of humanity. Although the Mosaic Law applied only to the Israelites, the moral components of the law were seen to be universally applicable.[26] Thus people are viewed as being free to obey or disobey God. Obedience to God's standards is seen as ethical conduct whereas disobedience is seen as unethical or immoral. This is the result of a theistic ethical system where ethics are derived from the Creator.[27]

Kaiser makes another point about the relationship between a person's intentions and actions as they related to ethical conduct. He describes how the Old Testament frames ethical action to include motivation or intention. Therefore the intent of the person becomes as important as the actual action the person engages in.[28] Thus it follows "that a norm forbidding killing is not a norm that applies only when an agent is motivated by hostility, hatred, or anger. Killing is impermissible also when it is motivated by the best of intentions."[29]

Hence when viewing abortion from a theistic ethical absolutist position the conclusion becomes obvious. God is the giver and sustainer of life. Therefore, to kill the unborn child for any reason other than self-defense, is wrong and misguided. For only God has the right to decide when to take life as the life that was given belongs ultimately to God. For a human being to determine when a person should die based on his or her own subjective methodology is always improper as it fails to recognize both the existence of absolute moral standards and the authority of God. Since God's Word describes human life and personhood as beginning at conception, then terminating the life of any human being from conception until natural death would be considered improper, or murderous. The only exception that God allows is in the case of self-defense or as just punishment when a person takes another person's life and the government chooses to carry out the sentence.

Having examined the concept of worldviews and the two predominant ethical views it becomes apparent that as long as differences exist in worldviews the abortion matter will remain a debate. Through persuasion and reason it is possible to arrive at a consensus but only after an initial consensus can be reached as to which worldview should be the standard for establishing the guide for moral decision making as it pertains to abortion. Despite the scientific evidence supporting the theistic worldview, adopting theism means humbling the self. Hence, abandoning an alternate world view which places the self as sovereign over the world often becomes an emotional not an intellectual struggle.

Chapter Five
Decision Making

A priest is charged with financial mismanagement and abuse of a congregation member. Police officers are charged with fabricating evidence and corrupting the justice system. A teacher is charged with engaging in a romantic relationship with one of her students. How is it that people who spend their lives teaching one thing reach a point where they choose to do something in direct contradiction to everything they believe? Can we ever hope to understand the mechanisms that underlie decision making, especially those decisions that are viewed as improper or immoral? Surely possessing faulty beliefs is not a sufficient answer as the examples above demonstrate that people often choose to do things that are contrary to their deeply held beliefs.

When it comes to immoral decisions, the Bible teaches that it is the propensity towards sin that is responsible in directing people towards immoral choices. However true it may be that sin lies at the very root of improper decisions, sin alone as an explanation does little to assist people in making better decisions, or in counseling people to make the best choices for their lives. Examining the space between the root of sin and the fruit of a bad choice will be the focus of this chapter.

Biblical Decision Making

Let us begin with the biblical text to set the frame for this investigation. It was previously mentioned that people possess a propensity to sin which is present at the time of conception. This current sinful nature continues to be present within each human until the time of the person's earthly death. Although the Bible describes a time in the future when this sin nature will be done away with for good, we have not yet reached that time in history. Thus as people, we are now infiltrated with the sinful nature which permeates all of what we do, think, and decide.

Despite this sinful nature, all is not lost. God has given us His revealed truth in the Scripture. The Bible contains all of God's moral will and thus can serve as the ultimate moral guide and authority for people. Since the Bible is the word of God and God does not err, the Bible serves as the inerrant authority on all matters to which it speaks regarding human living, including human decisions pertaining to moral matters.

In addition, God has given everyone who trusts in Jesus for the forgiveness of sin the Holy Spirit who indwells each believer to provide direction and to empower the believer to overcome sin in his or her life. This creates a spiritual tug-of-war within each Christian; he struggles with doing what he knows he ought not do while he often fails to do what he knows he ought to do (Rom. 7). For the unbeliever, he does not have the assistance of the Holy Spirit, and is thus left without this divine guidance. But knowing that God uses His Word and His Spirit to direct the affairs of people, it becomes certain that, "God will never lead you to do something that He has forbidden by His moral will in the Bible."[1]

Given what God has provided to direct human decision making, the following conclusions can be drawn to serve as an overarching context for how to approach decisions from a biblical perspective.

1. In those areas specifically addressed by the Bible, the revealed commands of God (His moral will) are to be obeyed.

2. In those areas where the Bible gives no command or principle (nonmoral decisions), the believer is free and responsible to choose his own course of action. Any decision made within the moral will of God is

acceptable to God.

3. In nonmoral decisions, the objective of the Christian is to make wise decisions on the basis of spiritual expediency.

4. In all decisions, the believer should humbly submit, in advance, to the outworking of God's sovereign will as it touches each decision.[2]

Again, these biblical principles serve as guides for the decision maker but do not necessarily prescribe how people go about making decisions or if people will even entertain the above principles when approaching decisions in their lives. Although it is somewhat counter-intuitive, expressed beliefs tend to be less accurate in predicting what people will actually decide to do when compared to actuarial models based on a person's demographics and prior life choices.

People do not necessarily act in accord with their expressed beliefs. Although expressed beliefs may play a role in the behavior that is ultimately displayed, understanding a person's beliefs may be less important in predicting behavior than understanding their mental processes and utilizing other preferences and behaviors that a person displays. In accord with this concept is the rise over the last couple decades of computer based models which have been used to accurately predict the behavior of people. These models have been used success-fully to predict what people will decide when voting, when making purchases, and when making relational decisions pertaining to divorce. In fact, it has been found through numerous research studies that actuarial models are more accurate in predicting behavior than individual people are.[3]

The field known as predictive analytics, in which vast amounts of preference and behavioral data are analyzed by computers to predict the future behavior of people, is now growing. Although predictive analytics holds a wealth of potential for research and simple behavioral prediction, it serves the task of predicting a behavioral choice far more so than understanding how a choice is made so that the particular person can be persuaded to choose differently. This latter concept is what will be examined at this time. To do so requires examining what the research has shown regarding what factors influence decision making in people.

The Research on Decision Making

The behavioral and social research have identified a number of different factors that influence decision making. Some of these are external factors, such as the situational or social context, while others are factors internal to the person, such as his or her sense of self-identity. By examining how these various factors influence decision making it becomes possible to develop some strategic approaches that will support people faced with making these decisions.

Social Factors

Researchers investigating decision making have often commented that decisional behavior is irrational when people do not act in accord with what is deemed ideal. However, Averbeck argues that although the behavior might appear to be irrational, it may in fact be viewed as being ecologically rational.[4] What this means is that the situational factors might actually alter what is considered ideal and therefore the environmental context must be analyzed to determine the rationality of decisions made in each circumstance.

Evidence supporting this position is derived from research conducted which involved looking at how people responded to social cues from others. The research involved having individuals attempt to learn which of two faces, the same person making either a happy face or a sad face, was associated with a higher rate of reward in a selection task. Researchers found that the happy faces were selected as being associated with a higher rate of reward on the experimental task even when this was not the case based on the actual experimental reward schedules. In fact the participants overestimated the rate of reward with the happy faces and underestimated the rate of reward with the sad faces. This research study concluded that the participants' decisions were a composite of social and utilitarian factors and that people are unable to decouple decision making from its social context.[5]

Additional support for environmental or situational factors

influencing decision making is found in a study by Cohen, et. al. This study sought to determine the extent to which situational cues could activate different motives within a person which ultimately would affect the person's behavioral decisions. This study utilized the classic prisoners' dilemma task where participants are to determine if they will cooperate with a partner for mutual benefit or seek to do what is best for themselves alone.

The prisoners' dilemma involves two individuals who are faced with a situation in which acting in accord with their own best interests results in a less than ideal outcome. The dilemma is framed as involving two people who have committed a crime. As they are both interrogated in separate rooms both of them face the same scenario. If both people betray one another by testifying as to the other's guilt, then they each will get a two year sentence. If one person betrays the other person and the other person remains silent then the one remaining silent will serve three years while the one who testified will go free. Lastly, if both remain silent then both will serve only one year on a lesser charge. Thus it serves both participants to cooperate and remain silent to achieve the guaranteed best outcome, as if each acts in accord with his own self-interest the outcome will be worse for each of them than if they had cooperated.

In this particular study, the prisoners' dilemma was presented with two different names. In one condition it was presented as the Wall Street game while in the other condition it was presented as the Community game. When presented as the Wall Street game only a third of the people cooperated with their partners. However, when presented as the Community game, seventy percent of the participants chose to cooperate with their partners. The researchers concluded that the social cues, in this case, the images tied to the two names given the prisoners' dilemma, led to cooperative behavior at different frequencies. This was explained as resulting from the impact of context on the participant's identity. "The same displays of steadfastness would be integrity-threatening in contexts that make salient one's identity as a level-headed negotiator or cooperative member of the larger community."[6] Thus, it was demonstrated that mere social context alone can have a dramatic impact on behavioral decisions.

Cognitive Effects and Decision Making

It has also been observed that how information is presented can impact decision making. The manner in which information is presented is known as framing, and framing has been noted to exert a powerful influence on decisions which are made. "McNeil et al. (1982) found that both physicians and laypeople altered the choice of surgery or radiation therapy as a treatment for lung cancer depending on whether likely outcomes were described in terms of survival rates or mortality rates."[7] This research demonstrates that people do not just evaluate the facts but rather the facts are evaluated differently depending upon how they are presented or framed to the hearer.

Another factor that impacts decision making is known as the endowment effect. This is the phenomena of a person experiencing the value of an item as increasing when it becomes part of a person's own property or endowment.[8] Interestingly, the endowment effect is not limited to material things. This effect is also observed with ideas. When a person takes ownership of an idea he tends to value it more than he should and often has trouble letting go of the idea even when evidence may suggest that the idea needs to be altered. The endowment effect has been used to describe how rigid ideologies come about as a result of the difficulty of giving up one's deeply held beliefs.[9]

Similar to the endowment effect is the disposition effect. This effect can be described as the observation that people tend to be more sensitive to losing things than they are to gaining things. People generally do what they can to avoid losses which are perceived as aversive while striving for gains. However, the disposition effect describes how the experienced magnitude of losing something seems greater than the magnitude of gaining the same item.

There have been attempts to integrate the various factors that influence decision making into various theories of decision making. There are two popular models which often are compared in the research. The first is the Expected Utility theory which tends to utilize a linear approach to decision making, and the second is the Prospect theory which posits that a nonlinear model is necessary to best explain decisions that are made.

Expected Utility Theory and Linear Theories

When attempting to determine the best theory, each theory must have its predictions examined. The best theory will be the one that makes the most accurate predictions. The Expected Utility theory states that people tend to evaluate the expected utility or value of each choice based on their perceived probability of obtaining certain outcomes. As a result of this analysis, the person will choose the option with the highest expected utility. However, "...psychologists' experiments have repeatedly shown that subjective expected utility theory is not a valid descriptive theory of human behavior" as people do not function in their decision making as would be expected if they were perfectly rational and analytical.[10]

Along the same lines as Expected Utility theory are the motivational theories of decision making. These theories which are also linear in nature, posit that the choices people make are the result of a compromise between two competing desires. This is similar to expected utility but does not involve calculating percentages based on one's expectations. Generally the motivational theories are framed in terms of selecting one outcome which is seen as the option that maximizes gain, while attempting to minimize the consequences of making a poor decision that would lead to the development of negative feelings of failure or disappointment. Larrick describes how it is the tension between these two motives that pushes decision-makers toward a specific level of risk seeking behavior. He discusses how people are different and that some people are actually far more concerned with avoiding failure than they are with achieving.[11] This is where the traditional motivational theories fail to account for decisions that people make, as the traditional theories suggest that people will opt for the decision that yields the greatest gain for the person but often this is not the case in actual experience.

One last theory which is similar to Expected Utility theory due to its linearity is the Crisis Decision theory which suggests that, "People consider the resources required to engage in a response and the direct and indirect consequences of each response option to determine the best response."[12] This is a theory that suggests that when two choices are available that it creates a crisis which must be resolved by weighing the good versus the bad and then going with the decisional avenue which maximizes the good for the person. Sweeny's conclusion about this theory is that when, "people evaluate their response options, they must select a response to the negative event by weighing the pros and cons of each response. In general, research has shown that people select responses that minimize cost and negative consequences and maximize benefit and positive consequences."[13] This is a linear approach of simple addition between good and bad and has hedonistic presuppositions in that the belief is that the person will choose based on what is best for him or herself.

Prospect Theory

Although popular for many years, the linear utility theories have come to be replaced with nonlinear theories of decision making. The best known is the Prospect theory which states that people making decisions, especially those which involve risk, do not do so in a linear manner. Rather, a reference point is chosen and from this point determinations are made regarding gains and losses. This theory states that people tend to be averse to loss and prefer to choose options which offer a lower perceived probability of loss. Additionally, people tend to select options, pertaining to gain, which offer the perception of a certain gain. People prefer a higher probability that they will get a little in terms of gain rather than a lower probability of getting a lot.[14] However, this process does not take place in a linear manner. Rather as the probability of loss increases as a person moves from his reference point he becomes disproportionately less likely to select that choice. Likewise, the same holds for selecting choices where the probability of gain increases from the person's reference point.

The reference point according to Prospect theory is derived from the person's status quo. Hence, people analyze choices from their status quo or current circumstances for determining losses or gains. In actual terms, according to this theory, for gains people desire a sure thing over a risk between nothing and a larger amount. For instance, a person would prefer to be given one thousand dollars over the option to be given a fifty percent chance of winning five thousand dollars and a fifty percent chance of winning nothing.

The reverse holds for losses as people prefer the risk of losing nothing or a larger amount over taking a certain loss. It has been demonstrated that people would rather choose the option of a twenty-five percent chance of losing one thousand dollars and a seventy-five percent chance of losing nothing over a sure loss of one hundred dollars.[15] Again, as the amount of loss or gain moves away from the person's reference point, his or her current circumstances or status quo, the impact of the loss or gain diminishes in the impact it has on the decision itself.

Although the nonlinear Prospect theory seems to better explain decisions that are observed in laboratory settings, this theory is still not sufficient in explaining actual decisions made in real life. Thus, there must be other factors at play rather than mere probabilistic calculations based on an underlying algorithm. In fact, there is voluminous research which has discovered that cognitive factors significantly impact decision making perhaps more so than rational probabilistic calculations.

Cognitive Dissonance

Cognitive dissonance is the theory of cognitive functioning which was proposed by Leon Festinger in 1957. This theory of cognitive functioning proposes that people try to reduce or avoid inconsistencies in their cognitive experience.[16] This manifests in the beliefs they hold, their perceptions of the world, and their behavioral decisions. Once a person has a certain expectation or belief about himself it is hard for him to incorporate new information which is dissonant or at odds with his currently held belief. One application which was developed by Aronson involves detailing how cognitive dissonance can be used in persuading and altering a person's attitudes.

1. If you want someone to form more positive attitudes toward an object, get him to commit himself to own that object.
2. If you want someone to soften his moral attitude toward some misdeed, tempt him so that he performs that deed; conversely, if you want someone to harden his moral

> attitudes toward a misdeed, tempt him – but not enough
> to induce him to commit the deed.[17]

In the first instance, once a person has decided that he wants something he will have a harder time criticizing it and thus will tend to over-inflate the positive qualities of the object. This also holds true with beliefs. This is demonstrated in the second example. It is suggested that once someone engages in a moral misdeed that he will be more likely to soften his attitude towards the misdeed. This results again as a result of the person's attempt to explain his past behavior. If he engaged in the behavior then it certainly could not be "that bad" and thus he softens his attitude against the misdeed. In the situation where the person resists the misdeed, he can then increase his belief that the behavior is indeed terrible, so terrible in fact that he was able to resist engaging in such behavior.

Cognitive dissonance aligns itself with Prospect theory in that the referent utilized by the person making the decision is based on the person's perception of him or herself and his or her circumstances. This is a subjective referent for decision making as each person will be different and the position adopted at one point in life is subject to change as the person's life progresses. This is in stark contrast to decision making which utilizes an absolute standard which remains constant at all times and in all places. However, when using a subjective standard, one's behavior becomes part of one's life experience and as such is incorporated into the subjective standard by which all behavior is judged.

Researchers have discovered that changes in behavior have been found to change the way people think about their behavior. In fact, their attitudes about their behavior actually change based on their conduct.[18] Again this is an example of how people try to make themselves the referent for decision making while illustrating the detrimental impact of choosing poorly as subsequent poor choices become more likely.

An example of this is found in the process of informal debate among people. To prove a point, people often resort to citing evidence to bolster their argument. Doing so is like engaging in inductive reasoning of sorts as each person brings forth what he believes proves that he is right. However, often the evidence is not evaluated by an objective standard and hence each person believes they have brought the weightier evidence to the table. Ultimately, each person likely concludes that he has the proper point of view. In actuality, what is likely occurring is a cognitive dissonance feedback loop where evidence consistent with the currently held belief is presented, which in turn further strengthens the person's belief. Evidence presented by the other person which may be contrary to the person's belief is quickly dismissed as irrelevant or wrong and thus the current belief is strengthened further.

Selective Perception

Cognitive dissonance focuses on what occurs in terms of the cognitive thought processes and beliefs a person holds. But research has also demonstrated that people also experience selective perception. This means that what a person actually perceives from his environment is limited by his beliefs. This is more than just superficial evaluation and dismissal. This is akin to wearing blinders to any information contrary to current beliefs and results in a person being significantly biased. As Sweeny says, "People who are motivated to come to specific conclusions engage in biased information processing that allows them to confirm their desired beliefs."[19]

It is one thing to perceive what is desired but the research shows that people can also be unconsciously conditioned to selectively perceive information from their environment. The cognitive and motivational factors responsible for selective perception can lead to a lack of awareness of critical elements in decision making.[20] People may truly be blind and unaware of what is going on and what is currently being presented to them based on their past experiences, their desires, and current beliefs.

Recognizing the impact that cognitive dissonance and selective perception have on a person's information processing allows the research on the disconnect between a person's behavior and his or her beliefs to begin to make sense. Research has demonstrated that people report that they often would act in ways that depart from how they believe they should act in any given circumstance. One study examined mental health professionals who were surveyed regarding their ability to evaluate what should be done in accordance with their ethical guidelines. These professionals reported that although they knew the guidelines, they were not always willing to implement decisions in accord with the guidelines. Their responses indicated that their actual behavior was affected by a wide range of factors apart from the ethical guidelines including their personal values and practical considerations of the situation at hand.[21]

These findings are somewhat puzzling in light of how the professionals expressed the desire to follow the guidelines and cognitively would have affirmed such guidelines as being part of their professional obligation as mental health practitioners. However, this study illustrates how human decision making is not as simple as the decision theories proclaim.

The Importance of Affirmation

In another study, it was demonstrated how individuals, when presented with information without any self-affirming statements in a situation, tended to accept those beliefs or statements that were consistent with their beliefs and values while becoming more polarized when exposed to mixed evidence. By contrast, individuals who were instructed to reflect on an important personal value, such as their relationships or who received positive feedback regarding one of their skills, tended to be more open to identity threatening information.[22] This study illustrates how mere affirmation of a person can alter his ability to perceive and evaluate new information which may be contrary to his currently held beliefs. This also suggests that a person's sense of identity plays a significant role in how he processes and perceives information when faced with a decision.

The authors of this study concluded that affirming a person's identity tends to reduce the importance of that person getting his or her way in a negotiation situation. Hence, the source of people's motivation tends to be to defend their identity rather than being motivated by an attempt to be rational or to maintain cooperative relationships. An interesting conclusion drawn by the researchers is that people assume their beliefs to be more valid and objective than alternative beliefs and thus when people are told to be rational they often perceive this suggestion as telling them to use their existing beliefs when evaluating new information.[23] In other words, this is the influence of pride at work in a person's life.

Thus, as people feel threatened they become less able to perceive information objectively as their cognitive filters are enacted as a self-defense mechanism. But thoughts and behaviors being linked means that behavior will also be impacted when a person feels threatened. "In particular, people who are vulnerable to threats to their self-image behave in ways that protect them from unfavorable information about their decisions."[24] This is exactly what cognitive dissonance and selective perception theorists would predict in terms of how biased beliefs would manifest behaviorally.

Self-Image and Decision Making

Other theories of decision making focus not on how people try to protect their sense of self but on how people attempt to protect themselves from experiencing regret. It has been assumed that people with low self-esteem are more vulnerable to threats to their self-image and thus are more apt to defend themselves against any potential threat such as a poor decision. This was discussed previously in light of how perception and behavior are altered when people feel vulnerable. However, people with high self-esteem can have decisions turn out poorly and they tend to be less sensitive to viewing a poor outcome as a threat to their self-esteem, and as such maintain their positive sense of self despite the negative outcome their decision had.[25] In fact, those people who are not feeling threatened are in a far better place to objectively evaluate not just the circumstances but their own beliefs as well. This has implications for helping people to make good choices especially since the research shows that people tend to utilize their experience and beliefs to determine what is rational and proper.

This tendency of people to make themselves the reference point for morality and truth is illustrated by the research just discussed. However, believing something about the self does not mean the beliefs will translate into action. Abstract opinions such as the importance of helping others or acting fairly to people of all races have been shown to at times be "at extreme variance with actual behavior."[26] What this means is that people have the ability to state what they would like or expect themselves to do in a certain circumstance, but that this stated expectation may have little to do with actual behavior.

One factor which increases the likelihood of action is the perception of the level of accountability. Those making decisions tend to be influenced to the degree to which they see themselves as accountable for the decision.[27] This is best illustrated by the mob effect when a person who is alone is more likely to help another individual in need than when the former is in a large group of people.

Still this does not explain how people who are by themselves make poor decisions for which they feel responsible and which go against their beliefs. Rather, it appears that there are emotional issues that seem to transform the decision making process from the desired rational approach to life to the often times irrational and reckless process which is observed. One author describes his own observations of his attempts to make sense of his decision making process.

> *This experience taught me that sometimes we want our decisions to have a rational veneer when, in fact, they stem from a gut feeling— what we crave deep down. I suspect that in our attempts to make sure that we end up with decisions that seem well-reasoned and thoughtful, we commonly undergo a lot of unnecessary mental gymnastics and justifications, particularly when the choices are large and significant.*[28]

In terms of what all this research means for understanding how people make decisions, it can be concluded that people generally want to perceive themselves in a positive light. Additionally people generally will make decisions that will bring them the greatest positive experience based on their expectations, their sense of self, and their current belief system. When it comes to helping people understand and follow God's revealed will the challenge to be faced is the contradiction that arises between the human tendency to make the self the referent and the biblical command to make God the referent for moral decision making. Unfortunately, people often act in accord with how they self-identify. But one positive outcome of this is that as people come to see their identity in biblical terms, or perhaps stated as their identity in Christ, that this will improve their allegiance to biblical values and to biblical behavioral decisions in general.

However, it should be noted that it is commonly believed that acting in accord with biblical values ought to feel good, but this often may not be the case. Living in accord with God's moral directives as revealed in His word will mean the denial of the self and recognizing the errors in thought and conduct that are inevitable in the human experience. Hence the momentary experience for the person embracing biblical living may be one filled with a certain level of frustration, unpleasantness, and internal conflict.

The Challenge of Subjectivity

From the research discussed so far it becomes evident that there are large individual differences by which decisions are made. Furthermore, it is necessary to consider a large number of factors which impact decisions as well as a person's ability to reason through or evaluate decisions that they encounter. Since people rarely choose things in absolute terms but rather rely on internal subjective values, predicting and making decisions becomes complicated because people do not have internal value meters that tell them how much things are worth or what is correct based on an absolute moral standard. Rather, people focus on subjective comparisons which reflect the relative advantage of one thing over another for themselves and then estimate the value of each decision accordingly.[29]

Since it is not possible to move away from the decisional process which is anchored in comparison, it becomes important to better understand the process that occurs when we decide between options. It is known that people tend to look for comparisons which are easily made and then proceed to choose the best of the similar options. As a result, we often neglect those options that are dissimilar or difficult to compare. This is one of the significant problems of subjectivity. Making decisions based on what one already believes means that new information will be excluded. Even worse is how subjectivity involves "making decisions on the basis of one's interpretation of inward impulses (feelings) and other 'road signs' that cannot be objectively verified."[30]

Hence subjective decision making will always be erratic as there is no stable foundation to evaluate decisional elements. Hence utilizing an absolute standard that remains constant in all places and at all times is necessary in order to truly determine which decisions are to be classified as good, bad, better, or worse. For those desiring to rely on the absolute standard of God's word it becomes evident that choosing an option outside of what God allows based on biblical revelation is always wrong as it goes against the parameters within which God has given us to operate and live.

Yet the research demonstrates that people tend to base their decisions upon their personal expectational systems, not just on external absolute standards. Thus, we base decisions on what we predict our future experience will be like if we make a particular decision not necessarily on what our future experience will actually be.[31] Since the biblical standard for moral decisions does not describe what the experience for the person will be like in the immediate moment of the decision, a person will have the tendency to rely on their own expectations and imagined conception of what the experience will be like.

Conflicts that develop which result from differences in desires, thoughts, and beliefs that a person has when compared to an absolute standard will lead to a sense of ambiguity in regards to the decisional process. It is known that people would rather eliminate risk rather than reduce risk as uncertainty creates stress. People experiencing stress may fixate on the first solution chosen, because having a solution is better than having no solution at all even if the solution is a poor one. This is one way that people decrease the anxiety they experience when faced with a challenging circumstance. As such, it could be said that high levels of anxiety lead people to search for solutions which may be just good enough rather than being optimal for the circumstances.[32]

This is yet another element that must be examined when evaluating the best decision in any given circumstance. As Rogerson says, "People are motivated to minimize regret and escape the discomfort of uncertainty and conflict."[33] As such, people tend to reject conflicting options or they may avoid making difficult decisions altogether. Related to this, people may attempt to avoid the ambivalence of a difficult situation and prematurely discontinue the active deliberation and make a hasty decision in an attempt to resolve a matter. This certainly can contribute to adverse consequences.

Emotions and Decision Making

Lastly, the impact that emotions have on decision making must be discussed. Of course, "ethical decision-making can be complicated when decisions involve complex situations, conflicting ideals, vague or nonexistent guidelines, and strong emotions." And, "We know that ethical knowledge does not necessarily result in ethical behavior."[34] A number of factors which help to explain this phenomena have been discussed but it must also be noted that emotions do impact decision making. This can occur from emotions that arise in the moment related to the circumstances, as well as emotions that are conditioned which lead to emotional responses that may influence decisions without our being fully aware of how we have been conditioned.[35]

Hardman proposes that the research on decision making suggests that we actually have multiple modes of decision making. He says that, "such results are consistent with the idea that two systems are involved in thinking: a deliberate, analytical system, and a fast, intuitive system."[36] Hardman discusses how the intuitive system which involves emotion can be overridden when a person is asked to provide reasons for the decision which is to be made. This suggests that giving more time to make decisions will increase the likelihood of making rational decisions. However, this is not always the case.

In life many decisions must be made quickly and unlimited time to contemplate a decision is not realistic for most of the decisions faced. This is consistent with the understanding that emotions impact decision making most significantly for those decisions that are chronologically proximal to the time of decision. However, the view that emotions are somehow a negative influence upon the rational mind has not held up under scrutiny, and some researchers have found that making quick decisions which are not thought out in some circumstances can actually be more accurate when compared to deliberate decision making.[37] Again this illustrates how common conceptions do not always hold true in real world living.

But this is not always the case. Emotions can in certain circum-stances influence decision making and lead to irrational and poor choices. One research study demonstrated that people are more likely to cooperate with smiling partners. "The results clearly demonstrate that the emotional expression on her face influenced the participants' decision-making."[38] It was found that participants in the study did show a bias toward selecting smiling faces in that they overestimated the number of positive outcomes attached to the smiling face that was used as a stimulus. Additionally, they underestimated the number of positive outcomes associated with both the angry face and the sad face that was presented as a stimulus item. The faces were of the same person just making different facial expressions so the researchers concluded it was the expression itself and not the attractiveness of the person utilized in the study. This has significance as it demonstrat-ed that even though there were elements that if analyzed in a purely rational manner would have led to different behavior, despite the available information, participants still based decisions on emotional cues.

This becomes most concerning when it comes to how emotions contribute to decision making involving sexual conduct. It has been determined by numerous research studies that "every one of us, regardless of how 'good' we are, underpredicts the effect of passion on our behavior."[39]

These studies found that across the board, people, when in an unaroused state, could not predict the behavioral choices they would make when they were in an aroused state. Participants consistently expected that their behavioral choices would be in line with those that they rationally knew promoted better health and relationships. However, once aroused, "Prevention, protection, conservatism, and morality disappeared completely from the radar screen. They were simply unable to predict the degree to which passion would change them."[40]

Hence it can be concluded that a far better strategy for those who want to guarantee that their behavior in the realm of sexual decision making is appropriate, is to teach strategies that involve walking away from situations that involve passion prior to being drawn in to situations that require restraining passion which has been shown to be woefully inadequate. The best approach is avoiding temptation altogether as this is far easier than trying to overcome it.[41]

Although emotions can be very useful in providing quick assessments in decision making, it is not enough to rely on emotion alone. Rather, emotions must be understood in terms of how they impact decisions and the power that emotions can exert in certain circumstances. Ultimately, any understanding of how decisions are made must incorporate emotions as the emotional experience is as much a part of the human experience as is cognition.

This chapter began with a discussion of the challenge involving truly understanding how decisions are made. Clearly it is much easier to state what a morally proper decision would be than it is to understand how a person comes to ultimately choose to do what is morally proper. Numerous theories have been put forth in an attempt to explain how people make decisions, but so far none have served as being fully adequate. Factors such as environmental and social cues, previously held beliefs, the way information is presented, and emotional experience all play a role in what a person ultimately decides to do. The chasm between knowing what God desires and choosing to do what God desires still remains fraught with challenges as people try to traverse this distance in their day to day lives. God has shared with people his desires in His word and He even provides empowerment and direction for those who have trusted in Him, but still people choose poorly at times. Even though it may not be possible to fully understand how every decision is made, it is possible to utilize what we know about decision making in an attempt to help support people to make the decisions that will ultimately be in their best interest.

Chapter Six
The Abortion Research

Given the length of time that easily accessible abortion has been legalized in this country, it is somewhat surprising that there is not more research examining how abortion impacts the lives of women. It has been said that over forty percent of women in America will have an abortion at least once prior to age forty-five.[1] Hence, when excluding miscarriages, approximately thirty percent of all pregnancies have ended in abortion since the ruling in *Roe v. Wade*.[2] This is a staggering number and yet many women in society have come to see an unexpected pregnancy as an even more shocking event. Who are the women who ultimately choose to abort their children and what impact does this choice in their life have on them? These are the questions that will be in view as the research findings are examined.

Understanding the impact abortion has on a woman's life is all the more important due to the frequency with which abortion occurs in America. An unexpected pregnancy certainly is a stressful life event. So what leads a woman to choose abortion as a response to this particular stressor? It has been said that personal circumstances more than personal beliefs and personal morality impact a woman's decision to abort. "Circumstances which lead her to choose abortion at one time may differ from those which lead her to carry a pregnancy to term at another."[3]

But studying external circumstances, or a woman's social context is insufficient. Personal experiences and thoughts, those categorized as being the subject of study in psychology, must also be examined to properly understand the abortion decision. As society has adopted the philosophy of self-esteem and self-gratification, a woman's perceived identity becomes an important factor in how she makes decisions for her life and by extension the life of her unborn child. "Women who have developed an identity that does not include being a mother may even react with catastrophic thinking characterized by feelings that continuing the pregnancy will 'end their lives.'"[4] Although this sounds rather alarmist, many women have come to believe that their life, their very purpose, is about pursuing the career they desire and often this means that children are not a part of the image of the life they see for themselves. Hence, it has been found that the "most common argument offered for an abortion was that continuing the pregnancy would jeopardize one's future."[5]

Putting the moral or ethical concerns aside for a moment, could it be possible that aborting an unwanted child could be the best thing for a woman in this day and age? Before answering this question, it will be necessary to first examine who the women are that tend to choose abortion. Then the impact on women will be examined because of the fact that "there is relative consensus among scholars in the field that at least 10-20% of women who have had an abortion suffer from serious negative psychological complications."[6] Although ten to twenty percent does not sound like much, when considering that a million and a half abortions occur each year in the United States alone it can be deduced that this means one hundred fifty to three hundred thousand women each year suffer serious negative psychological complications and this number does not include the number of women suffering physical complications.

To determine who the women are that tend to choose abortion, a number of research studies will be reviewed. Some studies look at the psychological factors while others look primarily at demographic characteristics. By drawing from the findings across studies a composite can be developed.

Who Chooses Abortion?

Demographic Characteristics

Most of the women who experience an unintended pregnancy tend to be in their teenage years or at an age when childbearing is not expected. This makes intuitive sense as women in these age groups are not generally focused on having children and expanding their family units. Coleman states that "approximately 77% of births to women over 40 and 86% of births to teenagers are the result of unintended pregnancies."[7] Thus, these two age groups are engaging in sexual relationships but due to their age they are not expecting a pregnancy. However, it seems that the older women choose abortion with less frequency than the young women.

Adler found in 1992 that the most frequent age group of women seeking an abortion is twenty to twenty-four years of age. Adler's review of the research determined that sixty percent of the women having abortions were under the age of twenty-five.[8]

A study conducted by Jones in the year 2000 of over ten thousand women found that, "21 out of every 1000 women of reproductive age had an abortion."[9] It was also found that women in the age ranges of eighteen to twenty-nine, who are unmarried, black or Hispanic, or who are economically disadvantaged have higher rates of abortion. Of particular interest is that of the women who responded to this survey, 42.8% were Protestant and 27.4% were Catholic.[10] It can be concluded that age alone does not explain the abortion choice. Rather, it would appear that age, ethnicity, and economic status all have some influence. Yet, the majority of people choosing to have abortions belong to religious groups which speak out most strongly against abortion.

A survey does not explain what causes women to have abortions, but it does describe who is choosing to abort their children so that further research can be done. Jones concluded that, "Information gathered from this nationally representative sample reveals that the typical woman having an abortion is between the ages of 20 and 30, has never married, has had a previous birth, lives in a metropolitan area, and is economically disadvantaged and Christian."[11]

When the reasons women give for having an abortion are examined most of them are consistent with the developmental stage associated with the teenage years and young adulthood. Some of the most commonly cited reasons for choosing abortion are concern for how the child would impact their life, not being able to afford a baby, and not being ready for the responsibility of raising a child.[12] Thus these reasons tend to reflect the high proportion of women who are young and have often not established their careers and families.

It has also been found that the frequency of abortion utilization is different across different ethnic groups. White women tend to have the lowest rate of abortions while Black women have the highest rate which is 3.1 times that of White women. Women of other races such as Pacific Islander, Asian, or American Indian fall in the middle with a rate two times higher than White women.[13]

Additionally, where a person lives seems to impact the frequency with which abortion is chosen. Women in metropolitan areas have significantly higher rates of abortion than do women in rural areas. This is consistent with the research findings that indicate that women in metropolitan areas are more focused on education and careers than rural women. Thus, the metropolitan women may see pregnancy as interfering with their personal goals to a greater extent than women in rural areas.[14]

However, the difference in abortion rates between metropolitan and rural areas may also have to do with the availability of abortion services. As the number of abortion facilities has decreased, there are now very few providers of abortion in rural areas with most abortion clinics and providers being located in larger metropolitan areas. Hence availability of and access to abortion services may be a significant factor in the greater number of abortions for women living in metropolitan areas.[15]

Not surprisingly, marital status is highly correlated with abortion rates. "Most abortion patients (82%) are not married; 63% have never been married. Estimates of age-adjusted abortion rates among women who are separated, divorced, or widowed are approximately four to five times the rate of women married and living with their husbands."[16]

It should be noted that despite the common cultural proclamation that living together is really no different than being married, Adler's review of the research suggests otherwise. Adler found a significant difference in the rates of abortion in unmarried cohabiting women when compared to married women who were living with their spouse. In fact, "Women cohabiting with men had abortion rates estimated to be five times greater than the overall abortion rate and nine times greater than that of married women."[17] Regardless of what the current culture desires to espouse, the research does indicate that legal marriage changes the family dynamics between a man and a woman, arguably creating greater stability and security.

Decisional Factors

Miller utilized the data from a longitudinal study which began in the 1970s of nearly a thousand women to try and identify antecedents to abortion. He found that women who were not married at the time of conception were much more likely to choose abortion. This finding is consistent with Adler's finding cited above. Miller also noted that this also included the group of women who expected their first or next child to be relatively far in the future. As such, this provides more insight into the finding that women who struggle with the concept of adjusting to having a child are more likely to seek an abortion if they don't believe they can adjust to the situation of having an unexpected child due to their marital status, the number of children they currently have, or if they are just not willing to put in the effort to change their perspective.[18]

Miller's research also focused on how the factors that are involved in the decisional process to abort a child are relevant. His findings are somewhat intuitive. Miller found that, "… the most salient finding is that the abortion decision process was significantly more complex (1) with a lengthier and more stable relationship with the sexual partner and when he was consulted about the decision, and (2) when employment was less salient to the individual." The second finding is not surprising in that if a woman is not as focused on her employment status then choosing to abort becomes more complicated as one of the primary justifications is now absent. However, the first finding that a lengthier and more stable relationship with her partner complicates the decision suggests that women possess the desire to raise children in a stable relationship. Hence with greater stability in the relationship, the choice to abort becomes more difficult as yet another major reason given to justify abortion is not present.[19]

Friedlander likewise found that, "The more involved the relationship, the greater its influence seems to be in the direction of continuing the pregnancy. Second, more complex decisions occurred when employment and career concerns were less salient. It may be that women who are strongly committed to employment justify abortion on those grounds; their decision is therefore less complex."[20] He goes on to conclude,

> *Our results suggest that while these two areas, "love and work," are critical in a woman's decision to use contraception and in her decision to terminate pregnancy, they operate differently. Strong partner involvement tends to encourage contraception yet complicates the abortion decision. Strong work commitment likewise encourages contraception but simplifies the abortion decision.*[21]

This research demonstrates that while many women seek to use contraception to prevent pregnancy, women in stable relationships, whose self-image is tied to their relationship, differ from other women in terms of their ability to integrate the role of motherhood when faced with an unexpected pregnancy. The woman who is in a stable relationship is able to more readily adjust her self-image to that of mother than the woman who is career oriented. Unfortunately a career and motherhood are perceived as incompatible for many women, and as such their unborn children find themselves in the middle of a seemingly unsolvable conflict. As is the case in many conflicts, the weaker party loses out – so is the case with the unborn.

It has been found that attachment plays a significant role in the abortion decision. There is a positive correlation between a woman's attachment to her unborn child and her choice to continue the pregnancy. Attachment and individualism likewise seem to go hand in hand in regards to choosing abortion. In 1984, Bradley completed a study of Canadian women who had recently given birth and found that, "…women with a history of abortion tend to describe themselves as self-reliant, independent, rebellious, and to enjoy being unattached or unconnected to other people, places, and things. Miller (1992) found that women who abort tend to be unmarried, independent-minded, and are likely to view abortion as both personally acceptable and as acceptable in the eyes of family members."[22] Hence, Western individualism does appear to serve as one factor in women choosing to abort their children. Dependency by a child is not seen as healthy or required due to the extreme individualism which now exists in the culture.

In fact, women who are less independent-minded, have been found to be less likely to choose abortion. Once a person is pregnant it requires an active decision to terminate the pregnancy as opposed to just being passive and doing nothing. Miller concludes that it is therefore presumed that more independent-minded women were more likely to make the active decision required to terminate the pregnancy.[23] Rather than attributing this to the fact that a woman who is not as independently minded is more relationally minded, the researcher concluded that the relationship between being less independently minded and choosing to continue the pregnancy was the result of passivity. This is the same error that occurs where Westerners judge Easterners as being passive due to their lack of self-assertion. However, after decades of cross-cultural investigation it has become clear that the Eastern cultural practices that do not emphasize the self are not founded in passivity but in familial relationship and obligation.

Perhaps the strongest predictor of abortion is what is referred to as the intendedness of the pregnancy. It has been found that almost one half of the conceptions that are not desired are aborted.[24] This means there is a strong positive relationship between the degree that the pregnancy is desired at the time of conception and the occurrence of abortion. Women who want children rarely abort. Women who do not desire to get pregnant, are at a much higher risk of choosing to abort their child. This is significant as the introduction of widespread contraceptive access and the espousing of the belief that people have the right to have sexual intercourse without the result of procreation means that people now view sexual relations as being detached from the reproductive function.

This was also confirmed by Miller's study which found that,

> *The lower the woman's childbearing motivation and the more effective she was as a contraceptor, the more likely she was to have an unintended pregnancy. This means that the greatest proportion of abortions occurred among those women who became pregnant in spite of motivation and behavior to the contrary.*[25]

This finding suggests that people truly believe they can separate the act of sexual intercourse from reproduction. However, the biological function of sexual intercourse is reproduction. With the advent of this separatist mindset people function in a near self-deluded manner relationally and then are shocked back into reality when the consequences of their actions are in line with the natural result of such actions. It is as if people have come to believe that what they will becomes truth and reality – in essence that they have become gods.

Motivation and behavior are closely tied in a person's functioning. This has been documented by other researchers as well. Lydon found that,

> *Commitment, in turn, predicted the decision to continue rather than to terminate the pregnancy. Moreover, the decision to continue the pregnancy (behavioral commitment) was associated with self-reported behavior (decreased smoking) that would facilitate a more successful pregnancy outcome.*[26]

Hence Lydon's research demonstrates that a person's commitment has widespread impact upon his or her behavior as a whole, and does not influence only a singular decision or aspect of his or her life. It is this reciprocal relationship between attitudes and behavior that was observed, and which Lydon concluded is a reflection of the dynamic nature of the commitment process in general. Attitude and behavior interact and as such the "…attitudinal commitment predicted pregnancy decisions, and in turn, the pregnancy decision bolstered attitudinal commitment."[27]

Women's Reasons for Abortion

Having reviewed the research regarding the demographic factors that are associated with higher rates of abortion, it is time to examine the reasons that women give for having abortions. It should be noted that first and foremost, abortion is now a choice for all women since it has become a legally protected procedure in this country. It no longer is an act of the desperate or criminal but is now promoted as a mere medical procedure utilized by women from all walks of life, and is often promoted as the most responsible choice available. It can be argued that legalizing abortion has had the greatest impact on the perception and frequency with which abortion occurs in this country.

It is Legal

People often equate what is legal with what is moral. Hence if a particular behavior is deemed to be legal then that behavior generally increases as more people no longer feel the restraint of the law upon them. Child abuse laws are a good example. Prior to having laws protecting children from abuse, parents would discipline their children in ways that would be considered abusive by today's standards. When legislation was passed people changed their discipline approaches to conform to the law. This pattern is what is observed in that people tend to conform their conduct to the governing laws.

As early as the 1960s, it was observed how changes in the law impact the frequency with which people opted to abort their children. Clyne, describing his experience as a medical doctor in England wrote, "Before the passing of the Abortion Act gynaecologists who conducted their practices on strictly ethical lines could seldom find good medical indications for the performance of therapeutic abortion where the life or health of the mother were endangered by pregnancy and would be improved by termination." He cited that the rate of therapeutic abortion for medical need was performed only once in every 16,750 deliveries. Clyne stated that due to the number of annual births in Great Britain, which was approximately 800,000, one would expect only forty terminations of pregnancy annually. He expressed concern because there were 22,256 therapeutic abortions in the last eight months of 1968.[28]

Miller likewise concluded that as long as women have unintended pregnancies and abortions are freely available as a way of resolving this problem in their lives, then women will make their choice by balancing their readiness to have a child and their feelings about the acceptability or rightness of abortion. He further expressed his belief that if abortion services became restricted this would offset the balance in the decision-making process and would significantly reduce the number of abortions performed.[29]

So both in England and in the United States it has been observed how the legalization of abortion has led to a dramatic increase in the frequency of abortion. The need to legalize abortion was promoted on the idea that abortion benefits women by protecting their health and improving their quality of life. However, it has been noted that "... amazingly, well-designed research specifically documenting how the procedure enhances women's quality of life is generally absent from the professional literature."[30]

Self-Interested Desires

It can be argued that abortion was not legalized to help women's health or their quality of life, but rather to further the philosophy that was spread in the 1960s that taught that self-gratification was the highest value and all other aspects of life must be subordinated to what each person chooses as being in his or her own best interest. This becomes clear when the reasons for why women have abortions are examined. One study done in 1987 found that,

> ... more than one factor had contributed to their decision to have an abortion; the mean number of reasons was nearly four. Three-quarters said that having a baby would interfere with work, school or other responsibilities, about two-thirds said they could not afford to have a child and half said they did not want to be a single parent or had

relationship problems.[31]

In this study done by Torres only seven percent of respondents indicated having only one reason which led to their decision to have an abortion. On average respondents cited 3.7 reasons for their choice to abort. Three-quarters said they decided to have an abortion because they were concerned about how having a child would change their life. About two-thirds said they could not afford to have a child. About half said they did not want to be a single parent or that they had relationship problems.[32] It was concluded that having an abortion was not a decision based on a singular reason for the vast majority of women. Rather, the decision resulted from weighing a complex set of reasons, which although different in nature, were all connected in the sense that the women in the study were concerned about how having a child would impact their lives.

The research investigating why women have abortions all seems to converge on a few similar reasons. They fall into a few categories. First, women choose abortion as they want to give priority to their career and education. Second, they are concerned about being able to financially support a child. Third, they are not ready for the responsibility of having the child. Fourth, their male partner does not favor having the child. Although the percentages of respondents who give these reasons varies a bit from study to study, these reasons were found to be the most common in nearly all the studies reviewed.

The commonality shared amongst women who choose to abort their children is that they are afraid of how having a child would change their lives. In fact, one study found that this was the most common reason given for abortion. "At all ages, the most commonly cited reason was that the respondent was concerned about the ways in which having a baby would change her life."[33] Two thirds of those who said they were concerned about the changes that would occur in their lives due to having a child expressed concern about how a child would interfere with their job or career. Almost half of these women said that having a child now would conflict with their schooling.[34]

Coleman noted that the decision to have an abortion was likely complicated when women were confronted with an unplanned pregnancy in the context of life situations that were not easily conducive to child rearing, such as when they were enrolled in school or in certain careers. Coleman also found that personalizing the child made it more difficult for women to have an abortion. This is consistent with the attachment research demonstrating that as women become more attached to their unborn child that abortion becomes more difficult for them to choose.[35]

Although the research is mixed, many studies have found that women who have abortions often do so because their husband or male partners desire the child aborted. Almost twenty-five percent of married women said they had been influenced by their husband's desire for them to have an abortion and more than one quarter of those women under the age of eighteen are influenced by their parents' wishes.[36] It appears that in an effort to please others, many women choose to abort when pressured by others to do so.

Sadly, it seems that many women view abortion as the lesser evil when compared to having the child or giving the child up for adoption. The research suggests that many women would rather have their child aborted than adopted. Although more research is needed in this area, it is hypothesized that many women see adoption as a personal failure which is ongoing, whereas they view abortion as a failure which occurs at a discrete moment in time. As such, women choose the event that they can control and which will be over most quickly. But this reasoning is flawed. And the research demonstrates that the decision to abort a child is not one that is discrete but rather has long term and serious consequences for the women involved in many instances. This is yet another example of how trying to do what is believed in the moment to be best for the self can lead to abortion.

Porter found that the women who participated in her study who chose abortion adopted a "utilitarian ethic" which was in conflict with their moral beliefs. The women felt they had to have the abortion despite feeling it was wrong.[37] This is a puzzling finding as it is often believed that people act based on what they believe is right or proper. Porter's research suggests otherwise. This is likely why she concludes that the *Abortion is Murder* campaign is ineffective, as all but one woman in her study believed abortion to be wrong and that it was the murdering of a child. This included the post-abortive women as well. However, the women still chose to have the abortion as they felt they had to do it given their circumstances. For the woman who chose to continue her pregnancy, the decision to not abort was not based on not wanting to kill her child, but rather on her belief that she could not cope with killing her child.[38] Again, this study illustrates that the locus of decision making is the self. The decision made is the one that is believed to best serve the self, not the decision that must be made to act in accord with morality, even the woman's own morality.

The observation that personal morality often does not alter a woman's decision to abort but rather her concern about personal discomfort if she chooses to abort, has implications for interventions which will be discussed later. However, these findings have led some to conclude that, "The multiplicity of reasons for choosing to have an abortion suggests that even if one specific problem is solved, it will not be enough to change most women's decision....This suggests that actions directed toward helping women who are unintentionally pregnant avoid abortion would be most effective if tailored to the individual."[39]

Financial Concerns

One of the primary reasons women give for why they desire to abort their child is financial difficulties. "Higher proportions of women who are unmarried or cohabiting, nonwhite, poorer and unemployed said they could not afford to have a child now, compared with the respective counterparts."[40] This study conducted in 2004, compared results with a similar study which was done in 1987. It was found that in 2004 seventy-four percent of women who had an abortion stated the reason as "having a baby would dramatically change my life", seventy-three percent listed the reason as "can't afford a baby now", and forty-eight percent listed "don't want to be a single mother or having relationship problems". These percentages were almost identical to the 1987 study.[41]

Thus financial concerns rank at the top for most women who choose to have an abortion. It has been previously stated that women tend to give many reasons for choosing abortion rather than having a single reason. The study conducted by Finer found this to be the case and when examining the pairs of reasons given, women included finances as part of their decision making in all instances.

> *Among women who gave at least two reasons, the most common pairs of reasons were inability to afford a baby and interference with school or work; inability to afford a baby and fear of single motherhood or relationship problems; and inability to afford a baby and having completed childbearing or having other people dependent on them.*[42]

Serrin Foster discusses how financial concerns are at the forefront for women choosing to abort their children. She argues that through various types of funding programs both governmental and private, that women can be supported when they become pregnant unintentionally. Ms. Foster advocates for the need to support women financially who are facing crisis pregnancies because abortion is not a choice that helps women but rather complicates their lives.[43]

Laura Hussey, in her 2006 dissertation research, investigated the extent to which social service funding impacted women and their decision to abort their children. Her research focused on trying to determine if more generous social welfare programs would reduce abortions. Hussey found that insufficient financial resources did tend to sway some women to have an abortion who were otherwise ambivalent towards abortion.

> *In contrast to the assumptions of previous research, however, women's responses to my survey suggest that even if economic need is not the only reason for choosing abortion, some women would choose otherwise if only they had access to assistance addressing that need. One particular policy remedy suggested by this project has been the expansion of child care supply in poor neighborhoods, but as it turns out, even socioeconomic disparity in this resource distribution is not so dramatic as envisioned, and will only go so far in affecting abortion incidence.*[44]

Hussey also discussed how women in both the abortion and childbirth groups expressed that there is a lack of understanding about how to access financial assistance. Additionally women in both groups expressed similar concerns regarding welfare assistance and support. However, of note is Hussey's finding that finances are nevertheless a significant overall reason in women choosing abortion. "Nearly a quarter of abortion patients professed that their lack of awareness about where to find help affording a child played a role in their decision, and several women in the childbirth sample also reported that they had considered abortion for this reason."[45]

Interpersonal Relationships

Women have historically been known as the caretakers of the family. Relationships tend to dominate the conscious minds of women. The propensity towards relationships was perhaps most starkly noted in the research which has been done on morality. Gilligan found that girls tended to view moral dilemmas in terms of relationships. Thus it should come as no surprise that Finer likewise found that women tended to be very relationally focused when it came to why they were choosing to either keep or abort a child. "Most women in every age, parity, relationship, racial, income and education category cited concern for or responsibility to other individuals as a factor in their decision to have an abortion."[46] What makes this a fascinating finding is it appears that the women who participated in this research study recognized the responsibility to other people, but for some reason either did not recognize the responsibility to the child in their womb, or they placed greater weight upon the responsibility they felt they had to other people.

Seemingly, the women in Finer's study have adopted a relational attitude toward their unborn children which would more traditionally be considered male in nature, being less concerned about others' welfare. This provides some evidence that the feminism of the 1960s and 1970s has indeed masculinized the feminine psyche, and now the consequences of this primarily male perspective are being witnessed. Additional evidence that women are acting in a more masculinized manner is manifested in their decisional processes. Historically women would have sought counsel from others whereas men have often made decisions independently. Finer's research demonstrates that women have indeed come to act far more consistently like the traditional male than the traditional female.

> *...our findings attest that women independently make the decision to have an abortion. The proportion of women citing influence from partners or parents is small (and has declined since 1987), and fewer than 1% of respondents indicated that this influence was their most important reason.*[47]

These findings are consistent with other research which found that almost sixty percent of women did not consult with the father of the child prior to having an abortion. Additionally, over eighty percent stated that the father of the child did not have any significant influence on their decision to abort their child.[48] Thus, despite prior research which demonstrated the influence of the husband or male partner over a woman's choice to abort, it would appear that there is a trend in which women are making the decision to abort far more independently in this era.

Paige Cunningham discusses how the lack of interpersonal support that is available to women in today's society contributes to the high rates of abortion. She discusses how research has indicated that many women who have had abortions would have chosen to keep their child had they been able to obtain the support they needed to continue the pregnancy as well as to continue their life plans. This is important given so many women who have abortions state that the choice to have an abortion was necessary so that they could accomplish what they desired for their life. If these women could still pursue educational and career goals while simultaneously having and rearing children, the need to terminate the children would be removed. Cunningham also noted that many women stated that a primary reason for having an abortion was that they did not have a friend who advocated for the pregnancy.[49]

Abortion's Impact on Women

In the 2008 review of the research conducted by the American Psychological Association's Task Force on Mental Health and Abortion, it was concluded that abortion does not cause any statistically significant impact upon women's mental health. The authors wrote, "The strongest comparison-group studies based on U.S. samples found no differences in the mental health of women who terminated a single unintended pregnancy compared with other groups of women once confounders were controlled."[50]

The results of the APA Task Force mirror those from a 1992 review conducted by Nancy Adler, et. al. The 1992 report found that "For the vast majority of women, an abortion will be followed by a mixture of emotions, with a predominance of positive feelings. This holds immediately after abortion and for some time afterward." In fact, other researchers found that women up to eight years after an abortion tend to continue to view their abortion in a positive light.[51]

Others have focused on the women who have had abortions. Those women who saw having a baby as interfering with other goals they had in life were found to experience better adjustment following their abortion decision.[52] In fact, it has been reported that "…the strongest feeling recalled in relation to the first three months after abortion was relief, with small to moderate degrees of guilt, anger, anxiety, and depression, and small levels of concern reported about future relationships and pregnancies."[53] Despite the fact that women reported some negative feelings after the abortion, Lemkau concluded that the abortion was not traumatizing, as the "… longer-term adjustment indicates very low levels of current distress or concern about the abortion. Reports of current relief, anger, anxiety, and guilt show lower levels of all of these affects than were recalled for the first three months after the abortion."[54]

Thus, abortion is seen as a benign procedure with minimal risks to the mental health of the woman undergoing the abortion. Based on the many research studies that have been done that demonstrate only mild and transient reactions to abortion, most researchers claim abortion is safe and necessary for women. Even most of the long-term effects which have been observed by some researchers are considered benign by the APA Task Force. Lemkau's reports serve as added evidence for the minimal impact that abortion poses on women's health. The findings have identified that immediately after the abortion and during the time the study took place, which was approximately on average nine years post-abortion, the women reported a very high endorsement of a woman's right to choose abortion.[55] Lemkau does not entertain the possibility that the women continue to endorse the right to choose due to cognitive dissonance and the resulting bind they would be in if they did not endorse such a right after their own abortion.

It seems that the majority of the researchers are finding no significant ill effects for the majority of women undergoing abortion. But the question that must be asked is why do some women continue to have symptoms, sometimes for years after a procedure which is supposed to be so benign? Additionally, what accounts for the puzzling research finding that demonstrates that women who adjusted reasonably well after having had an abortion were less likely to abort a future pregnancy even when faced with an unplanned pregnancy compared to women who never had an abortion in the past? Researchers concluded that, by virtue of having previously had an abortion, the subjects in their study rated themselves as being more committed to the current pregnancy. This led the researchers to determine that this finding suggests that having an abortion does have a longer-term impact on a person's thinking that has not yet been fully fleshed out in the research.[56]

Perhaps the lack of findings relates to the instrumentation that is utilized when assessing for mental health impact. Since the instruments are geared towards specific psychiatric symptoms, it would be possible that the psychiatric picture of impairment from abortion may not be identified with the current instruments being utilized. It seems certain that something is amiss with the findings published by the APA Task Force, as other researchers have found some startling results pertaining to the level of impact that abortion has on the lives of people who choose to terminate their child's life in this manner.

Coleman found that over one third of both men and women in his study reported that they sometimes wished they had not decided to abort their child.[57] This is a significant finding as it demonstrates that having an abortion indeed does have a longer term impact on the thinking of both the men and women involved.

Other researchers have found that those who are adversely affected after an abortion suffer symptoms that are akin to those that are stress-related and often are identified as anxiety, depression, substance use/abuse, sleep disturbance, and increased risk of suicide.[58] Along these lines are the studies that have found that future reproductive events often bring back thoughts and emotions associated with the prior abortion procedure, "...even among women who report no distress at the time of the abortion."[59]

This is significant as it illustrates how the results obtained in a research study are dependent on what research questions are asked and what instruments are utilized. If women are having future psychological reactions and emotional responses resulting from an abortion, even when they were found to have no distress at the time of the abortion, it should become obvious that something is being missed when the well-being of the woman is evaluated postabortion.

Other researchers have found that over eighty percent of women felt victimized by the abortion process with a large number of women feeling they had been coerced. Women who do choose abortion due to relationship pressures are especially at risk of feeling coerced.[60]

Even pro-choice author Miriam Claire describes how Mira Dana, a psychotherapist in London who has counseled women after they have had abortions, has said that women tend to have one of the three following reactions after an abortion. One, euphoria, two, detachment, and three, depression. "Not all women feel loss, anger, guilt, and depression after an abortion, as Mira Dana suggests, but some do, and most women certainly experience at least one of those feelings."[61]

Other mental health providers have commented that,

Quite apart from the guilt reactions analyzed by Ekblad and by Polonio and Figueirado, who found that at least 25% of women who submitted to legal abortion in Scandinavia bitterly regretted having done so subsequently, there is, I understand, evidence to suggest that women who undergo termination of pregnancy for psychiatric reasons where other treatment would be preferable may be left in a worse state than they were before.[62]

The reality is that there are numerous researchers who have found that there are actual negative mental health effects that result from having an abortion. Far more women are impacted by abortion each year than the pro-choice advocates promote. In fact, if the figure were only ten to twenty percent as most researchers agree, there would still be hundreds of thousands of women in society suffering as a result of abortion. If the numbers are higher as other researchers suggest, perhaps as high as thirty percent or more, then it becomes evident that millions of women in society are suffering from psychological sequelae resulting from having had an abortion. These women who are suffering are the mothers, wives, sisters, and daughters of our nation, not to mention all the men who also are suffering due to their involvement with abortion.

So how can so many researchers continue to claim that abortion is safe and very few people have any negative consequences? This author suggests that it is a matter of perspective. Much like the two people viewing a glass of water where one says it is half full and the other half empty, the way a researcher defines minimal impact can radically shape their research findings, conclusions, and recommendations. It is now time to examine the research to see what has been determined about who is most at risk for developing significant ill effects after an abortion.

Those at Greatest Risk

Just as the majority of women who have abortions tend to be young, in like manner, younger women are also more susceptible to experiencing post-abortion difficulties.[63] Even Adler, who is pro-choice, recognizes this as being evident when she says, "Younger and unmarried women without children are relatively more likely than those who are older and who have already given birth to experience negative responses."[64]

Other researchers have described the women most prone to post-abortion psychological problems as tending to have the following characteristics: low self-efficacy for coping with the abortion, low self-esteem, an external locus of control, difficulty with making the decision, having an emotional investment in the pregnancy, perceptions of one's partner or family members as unsupportive, being an adolescent unmarried or poor, having pre-existing emotional problems, having poor or insecure attachment with one's mother or separation from one's mother before age sixteen, involvement in violent relationships, traditional sexual orientations, and conservative views of abortion and religious affiliation.[65] Surprisingly, this list of characteristics also would seem to describe the very women who are most likely to have abortions according to the research. Putting these two findings together would suggest that the majority of women who have an abortion are likely to be suffering to some extent from the abortion experience.

Furthermore, as studies have shown that the majority of women having abortions are self-identified as Protestant or Catholic, it appears that based on their religious affiliation alone the majority of these women are at high risk for negative complications after an abortion. This is consistent with research which has found that "... women whose culture or religion prohibits abortions and those who attend church more frequently"[66] are at greater risk for negative psychological symptoms after an abortion.

Another significant factor in the likelihood of a woman developing psychological difficulties after an abortion is the recognition of the unborn as a person. It has been found that "Procedures done in the first trimester of pregnancy carry lower risks of physical morbidity and psychological difficulties than do second-trimester procedures."[67] When an abortion is done in the earlier stages of pregnancy it is easier for a woman to convince herself that the child is not human or not fully human, and thus the abortion is easier to justify. As the pregnancy progresses, and the child begins to be felt moving within the womb of her mother, it becomes far more difficult to nullify the child's humanity. Certainly later term abortions that are not performed by surgical removal but through killing the child by some means and then allowing the mother to deliver the dead child makes it very difficult to rationalize the abortion in the mother's mind. Seeing the dead child furthers the reality that the mother chose to end the child's life.

This has been confirmed by research as well. One interview based study by Patterson in 1995 "revealed that women who felt more of a bond to the fetus prior to abortion experienced more difficulty afterwards compared to women who did not feel such a bond. In this study, bonding tended to emerge as a function of the participant's awareness and embracement of pregnancy-related physical changes."[68] Just as previously discussed, as a woman's body changes in relation to the child growing within her, it becomes difficult for women to not become attached emotionally to the child. This is similar to the position that women often take that abortion is the lesser evil when compared with adoption. It is believed that mothers who give their children up for adoption suffer significant pain due to the maternal attachment formed upon delivery. Consequently, they see ending the life of the child in the womb before they are as attached as a better solution for them.

However, some researchers have suggested that there is consid- erable evidence of strong emotional attachment forming between the mother and child while the child is still in the womb. This means that having an abortion always runs the risk of leading to psychological distress as the maternal infant attachment is broken by the voluntary choice of the mother.[69]

> *Women who have had an abortion but who tended to believe that fetuses are human scored lower on the well-being variables than women who have not had an abortion. However, women who have had an abortion and who tended to believe that fetuses are not human were as well adjusted as women who have not had an abortion.*[70]

Conklin discussed how he believed that the enduring belief that the fetus is human may be due in part to the persuasive arguments from the pro-life campaign that has been going on for the last few decades. Conklin raised a valid point that a person's moral objection to killing another person can be overcome by redefining a person as inhuman. Hence, as the pro-life advocates have demonstrated with irrefutable evidence that the developing child is human it has had an impact upon society and people in general. Now the arguments about the humanity and personhood of the unborn are viewed not as irrational or inflammatory, but as persuasive.[71] The result of elevating society's consciousness about the humanity of the unborn will serve to also increase the number of women who suffer adverse effects post-abortion as they encounter the dilemma of having engaged in conduct counter to their moral beliefs.

This line of reasoning has been reached by others who say, "… findings suggest that there may be negative consequences for psychological well-being when inconsistent personal realities are not resolved." This is consistent with the research that demonstrated that when people saw the unborn child as human and they had an abortion they had significantly more psychological problems. Additionally, it was demonstrated that women who had an abortion and whose perspective was that the unborn child was not human were no different in terms of their adjustment than women who had not had an abortion.[72] However, as was discussed previously, the methods used to assess for impairment may not be sufficiently sensitive to properly detect the difficulties that women who have abortions experience.

Another factor that increases the risk of suffering significant psychological distress after an abortion is the amount of difficulty with choosing to abort.

Studies examining the relation between aspects of satisfaction with the abortion decision and postabortion emotional response consistently find that women who were satisfied with their choice or who report little difficulty in making the decision to abort, show more positive postabortion responses. Greater difficulty in making the decision has been associated with higher negative postabortion reactions.[73]

Other researchers have focused primarily on the consistency of the decision making process with the woman's personal values and moral view of abortion. Hoggart takes the stance that it really does not matter what a pregnant woman does as long as she chooses to do something that is consistent with her moral outlook. In essence, he describes the significant factor as the woman making decisions autonomously and in concert with her own self-determined sense of right and wrong.[74]

If negative outcomes were solely based on the consistency of the decision making process alone, perhaps Hoggart's perspective would hold some merit. However, the findings that there are numerous factors that contribute to a negative psychological outcome make Hoggart's position untenable.

Nevertheless, other authors join Hoggart in the attempt to proclaim that as long as a woman chooses based on her values she will be just fine. Adler says, "Studies that have included comparison groups of women who carry to term…suggest that the choice made by women regarding their pregnancy is the one that is most likely to be best for them." She further describes how women who were less conflicted and more certain of their decision seem to cope far better post-abortion than those who are conflicted or uncertain about their decision. This is the basis for Adler's conclusion that a woman who is confident in whatever choice she has chosen for herself is ultimately what is best for her.[75] Again, Adler like Hoggart, takes the position that each person can develop their own personal morality, and thus they are the determiners of right and wrong. However the evidence suggests that morality is not something that is individually created but rather is something that is given and then only individually accepted or rejected.

Additionally, Adler and Hoggart take the position that what is best for a woman is what is best in terms of her psychological well-being. However, the concern must be raised that utilizing psychological well-being as a standard is a very poor indicator of morality or ethical living. It can be expected that anyone who justifies their immoral conduct will have far less regret, guilt, and future psychological distress than those individuals who do not rationalize their immoral conduct. Rather, they understand that they have chosen poorly and that their conduct was wrong and improper.[76] Psychological well-being by itself is not sufficient as a measure of determining what is best. Alternately, all aspects of a person must be kept in view: the physical, emotional, psychological, and spiritual. When this holistic approach is adhered to, it becomes apparent that each person cannot merely decide what is right and wrong and do it – she must discern what is right and wrong from some source outside herself, the universal morality, and conform her life to this standard.

A counterintuitive finding related to decision making is that women who have received support from a male partner for their abortion tend to suffer more psychological distress over the long term. "At one year post resolution, a strong relationship with a male partner was associated with feelings of regret among aborters but was unrelated to regret among deliverers."[77] This would appear to be just the opposite of what would be expected. Yet, this finding has been consistently found as Lemkau also states,

> *An unexpected finding, one that contradicts the expected relationship between social support and post-abortion adjustment, was that those who consulted and received support for their abortion decision from their sexual partners had less favorable long-term adjustment than those who either had not consulted their sexual partner or had pursued abortion in spite of his opposition.*[78]

Studies in other countries have focused more on the impact that male partners have in terms of pressuring a woman to abort a child. A study done in Norway from a sample of women who had induced abortions in 1998 found that pressure from a male partner to have an abortion was most highly associated with negative psychological responses in the period after the abortion. It was found that these negative feelings continued at six months and two years after the abortion as well.[79]

These findings are consistent with the findings indicating that women who experience coercion when undergoing an abortion are more prone to developing psychological problems as a result.[80] However, even in the absence of coercion, those supported also had less favorable outcomes. When looking at these findings it appears that the research is finding that both women who are coerced and women who are supported by a male partner do more poorly psychologically after having an abortion.

It makes sense that women undergoing abortion would experience psychological difficulty given they are ending the life of a child that is developing inside of them. This is what Miller found in his research.

The loss response involves sadness, anger, and guilt. Miller's research determined that women who are ambivalent about the decision to abort are far more prone to experience regret about the decision in the future.[81] Thus, this research is consistent with what other researchers have found regarding ambivalence, and yet it adds the dimension of loss which is not typically addressed in the research. The existence of a loss experience indicates that the woman knows something is no longer present in her life. In the case of abortion that absence is her child.

The Health Impact on Women

The loss of a child may not be the only loss a woman faces after having an abortion. For many women a loss of mental and physical health occurs. It has been demonstrated how numerous researchers tend to downplay the mental health impact abortion has on a woman by focusing on those women who seemingly have no ill effects. The same is true in the realm of physical health.

It has been documented in the medical literature since the 1970s how carrying a child to full term delivery serves a protective effect on a woman's health. When a woman's normal pregnancy is disrupted through abortion it increases her risk of health problems. Dr. Shadigan describes these risks when she says, "…given a few methodological caveats, current research suggests that a history of induced abortion is associated with an increased long-term risk of: 1) breast cancer, 2) placenta previa, 3) pre-term birth; 4) maternal suicide."[82]

Other doctors have also reported the increased health risks associated with abortion. Breast cancer is one physical illness which certainly has received a lot of attention. Dr. Lanfranchi describes the physiological changes that occur during pregnancy and how inter-rupting a pregnancy by abortion interrupts the typical physiological changes that occur in a woman's breast during pregnancy. This creates a scenario which increases a woman's risk of developing breast cancer as the cells that undergo changes are most likely to cause cancer when they are in their early stages of development. An abortion stops the de-velopmental process and prevents the cells from reaching the mature stage, and thus a woman has an increased number of immature cells in her breasts which are far more prone to developing into cancer. The physiological activity in the breast that creates this increased risk has been well documented in experimental studies with animals and epidemiological studies in women.[83]

Thus abortion has been demonstrated in research studies to pose a risk to both women's mental and physical health. These risk factors are not generally discussed in the general dialogue about abortion, and perhaps if women understood the increased risks to their health then they would not be choosing to end the life of their unborn child.

The last area to examine in terms of the impact on women's health is the concept that somehow only those predisposed to mental and emotional difficulties experience negative effects after having an abortion. Again, the research does not support this claim.

Researchers in Denmark found substantially higher psychiatric admission rates in women who were separated, divorced, or widowed and who had terminated their pregnancies. The authors surmised that perhaps these individuals were more likely to be terminating pregnancies that were originally intended, which the research has shown places women at higher risk for having negative psychological reactions.[84]

In comparison to women who did not expect to cope well with an abortion experience, those who expect to cope well were reported to have less severe depressed mood and fewer physical complaints after an abortion and up to three weeks later.[85] However, this just means that some women are coping more effectively with a situation that requires coping with, namely the loss of their child through their voluntary choice. To say that some people are able to get through this experience with less distress does not really address the underlying issue which is that the abortion experience causes women to suffer.

The research data indicate that many women are experiencing some level of psychological distress after choosing to abort a child. Despite many researchers claiming that abortion has little impact on women's health, overall it still must be noted that there are hundreds of thousands of women each year who suffer serious psychological and physical impairment resulting from their decision to have an abortion. As early as 1992, only two decades after Roe, Zoelese and Blacker concluded that,

> *...psychological or psychiatric disturbance occurring in response to abortion may be characterized as marked, severe, or persistent in approximately 10% of women. In view of the fact that 21% of all US women of reproductive age opt to terminate unwanted pregnancies (Forest, 1987) and 1.5 million abortions are performed annually in this country, the "minority" frequently referred to in the literature translates into a sizable number of individuals suffering from ill effects.*[86]

The research, although mixed, still provides a clear picture that abortion is not an event in a woman's life that can be casually experienced. Rather, abortion has an impact on nearly all women who choose this for their child and many women experience significant emotional, psychological, and physical ailments as a result. Although abortion is often billed as being preferable to child birth and the associated stresses of child rearing, the research has not found this to be the case. In fact one study found that all the women surveyed who chose to have their child did not experience regret about their decision. However, all the women who chose abortion "expressed deep sadness, physical pain, and guilt...The young women did not feel 'free' from the pregnancy as anticipated. Instead, the feelings about the abortion experience replaced any positive feelings of relief following the surgery."[87]

In summary it should be noted that even the researchers who have taken the stance that abortion causes no significant increase in risk to women's health still acknowledge that many women still do have significant mental health problems after an abortion. "Abortion is an experience often hallmarked by ambivalence, and a mix of positive and negative emotions is to be expected."[88] Thus, as long as abortions are performed on women, women will continue to suffer the impact of abortion on their health. This means that hundreds of thousands of women each year will experience significant psychological disturbance, while many more will experience symptoms that perhaps do not rise to the level of a diagnosable condition, but nevertheless impact the woman's experience of life. This also does not take into account the millions of women who are now at an increased risk for numerous physical ailments, including breast cancer, because they have had a prior abortion.

Of course there will always be those people who can undergo an abortion and then continue on in life as if nothing has happened. But these exceptions do not prove the rule. Despite the pro-choice advocates and researchers arguing that abortion has no long term impact on women's health, the research suggests otherwise. Even the ardent pro-choice advocates admit that ten to twenty percent of women suffer significant psychological sequelae after an abortion. Again, this means that one hundred fifty to three hundred thousand women a year will be in need of mental health treatment resulting from their abortion. Even with hundreds of thousands of women being identified, the entire body of the research literature suggests this number to be much higher. Asking the right question is the first step in guiding research to get the right answer. The converse also holds true, for by asking the wrong question the researcher will get the wrong answer, or an answer not consistent with the reality of the circumstances. It would appear that the advocates for abortion want to find that women are not impacted, and thus define impairment in ways that fail to detect the suffering and loss that is inextricably tied to the abortion experience for a majority of women.

Chapter Seven

Implications For The Crisis Counselor

The many demographic characteristics of individuals who choose abortion, as well as the numerous reasons why abortion is perceived to be the best choice for many people have been discussed. However, now it is time to come to terms with what is driving the decision to abort a child. Gaining insight in this area will best serve the crisis counselor who often has minimal interactional time with a counselee. Being able to identify the core driving force for a person who is contemplating abortion and knowing how to address this with a counselee are truly the mark of a competent counselor.

The Fundamental Reason for Abortion

Worldview and Ethics

Numerous books have been written and many more people have opined that the cause of abortion resides in people adopting a faulty worldview or possessing certain ethical positions. If this were the case, then it would be expected that utilizing an approach incorporating rational analysis to compare the various positions would lead the person contemplating abortion to reconsider. For example, a counselor might discuss with a person how a utilitarian ethical system fails to offer the ideal balance of personal rights and benefits. By using a variety of logical arguments it could be demonstrated that adopting an ethical system based on absolute values would be more conducive to proper living.

Alternatively, the same could be done with comparing worldviews. Since the observable physical evidence, logic, and philosophical reasoning all support a theistic worldview, individuals adhering to other worldviews could be swayed to adopt the theistic worldview. Although this may be true, the question that must be asked is will altering a person's worldview or ethical system alter her decision regarding abortion?

It would seem that many authors believe this to be the case. Numerous books have been written examining the atheistic worldview which attribute this position to concluding that aborting a child is morally acceptable. Often authors conclude that the way to end abortion is to get all people to adopt the correct theistic worldview. Others argue that faith in Jesus would bring about a correct worldview. In essence, if people could only adopt the understanding that all people are created and are image bearers of God then the desire for abortion would decrease dramatically. Likewise it is believed that if people could adopt an ethical system which placed the value of life above their desire to increase what is perceived as the most beneficial outcome for themselves, that they would naturally choose not to abort their child.

Unfortunately, this is not what is observed. People who hold a theistic worldview as well as ethical systems which would rationally seem to oppose abortion, still choose to abort their children. It must be remembered that as many as three quarters of all women choosing to abort their children in the United States self-identify themselves as Christian. If all that was involved in stopping abortion was helping people to understand that there is a God, and therefore we as people do not have the right to take another person's life except in self-defense, then spending a few minutes to rationally work through the circumstance would be expected to result in the majority of women choosing to continue their pregnancies. However, this is not what is observed. It has also been stated that if people would approach the abortion decision rationally, they would not choose abortion. However, research has demonstrated that what people believe to be rational often is their own pre-existing thoughts. Thus, most people believe they are already acting rationally even when they pursue having an abortion. It is for this reason that it is unlikely that people will adopt a rational approach to solving even the simplistic problems that are faced in life.

Perhaps the best evidence that demonstrates that rational thinking is not the primary solution to prevent abortion is found in the decision making research. Crisis decision theory was discussed previously and it holds that people weigh the pros and cons and then make a decision based on what is in their best interest. Yet, this theory of decision making has not been found to apply to how people actually make decisions in their lives. Again, it sounds rational and hence seems to be an acceptable explanation, but in actual practice something else is driving decisions and it cannot be explained as a failure to adopt rational thought. Lacking rational thought seems to be endemic to being human, and therefore to seek a solution to abortion that requires rational thought as foundational is futile. If the world were different and people always chose what was rational from a logical perspective, then the world would be a very different place. However, it should be obvious that although much focus has gone into debating the merits of being pro-life or pro-choice, the majority of women will not be persuaded to continue their pregnancy due to being presented with a sound logical argument.

The Popular Reasons

Other authors have concluded that what drives abortion are a variety of social and circumstantial factors which can be distilled down into the concept of deficits. Lacking time, money, or desire to have a child tend to be at the root of the reasons given for women choosing abortion. If this were the case then those seeking an abortion need only be provided resources to bring about a change in their mind. If a woman did not have the time to raise a child, childcare could be offered to support the woman in pursuing a career or her education while raising a child simultaneously. If the expense of child raising was of concern, then monetary subsidies could be offered.

The problem with the belief of deficits being the core factor driving abortion is that even when such deficits are not present, women still opt to abort their children at a staggering rate. Many women who are wealthy, educated, and in stable families still choose to abort their children. Although women of lower socio-economic status, those who are single or cohabitating, and those with minimal social support choose to abort their children with greater frequency, the fact that women choose abortion in the absence of resource deficits suggests that deficits are not foundational in driving the decision to abort a child.

Egocentrism

What makes a person determine that their life is more valuable than someone else's life? The foundational answer to what drives a woman to choose her own life over that of her child is egocentrism or the belief that the world centers on the self. In simpler terms, it is selfishness. This is the mechanism that is the unifying factor underlying abortion. Rather than focusing on trying to win the mind by using well-built logical proofs or providing comfort by supplying any of the multitude of sociological supports, the abortion phenomena will best be addressed when it is viewed for what it is, the ultimate in human selfishness. This of course does not mean that appealing to a person's rational mind or offering to provide for her needs should not be entertained, just that these approaches will likely be met with limited success.

So how can selfishness be addressed? First, it becomes necessary to determine how a person's egocentric position is manifesting. Once the specific egocentric position is identified, interventions can be developed to ultimately address the emotional aspects of the person as emotions tend to drive behavior which is focused on the self. Lastly, by addressing the egocentrism in a person's life it becomes possible to appeal to her conscience. Appealing to the conscience is of utmost importance, for it will ultimately serve as the restraining force which can be used to persuade a woman to choose to continue her pregnancy.

Before examining how such interventions can be implemented, one example to demonstrate this conclusion will be given. A study was conducted to determine the effect of teaching rational decision making and skills development in the area of sexual decision making. It was found that a comprehensive educational program yielded limited success when it came to altering sexual conduct in adolescents. Those who were participants in the study continued to engage in sexual behavior which led to pregnancy and the risk of sexually transmitted diseases. Despite the education and skills training that was provided, the study participants continued to engage in sexual intercourse without contraception even when contraception was available to them.[1]

Rational thinking is often the first thing to be abandoned in a difficult situation. Resources that are provided often are not utilized, as the object of the person is to bring about her own gratification. In these circumstances, the person's mind and emotions merge and work together to bring about that which seems to result in the most immediate pleasure and relief. Hence, such decisions tend to be short sighted, and certainly not what would be deemed rational upon objective analysis.

This is the problem with women who choose abortion in response to an unwanted pregnancy. Women, and oftentimes their partners, do not want to be inconvenienced. The desire for self-pleasure or doing what makes them most happy and comfortable initiates a process which leads to viewing the unborn child as a problem. Objectifying the unborn human being makes it easier to rationalize the subsequent killing of the child but ultimately the killing is not done by what would be considered an infanticidal maniac. Rather, the woman is perceived by herself, and others who are like minded, as doing what needs to be done so she can have the life she wants. Interestingly, there have been a variety of factors which have made this rationalization easier, such as abortion being legalized. Nevertheless, choosing abortion requires rationalizing personal conduct that the woman knows is wrong. The vignettes in chapter one illustrate how women have abortions thinking it will solve a problem, but this is only possible through rationalizing their conduct. Once they have committed the act of killing their child they are faced with living with their conscience from that point forward. Thus abortion victimizes both the unborn child and the mothers and fathers who choose to put their children to death.

Intervention Strategies for Counselors

People don't change readily when they are being coerced to do so. This happens whether the pressure is external or comes from within. Threat, fear, and anxiety, regardless of source, will diminish one's ability to change. Many who wish to change are already vulnerable to threat because they harbor feelings of guilt and shame. Some have assumed a particular ideological stance because of deep underlying insecurities. A frontal, verbal attack against their belief system is likely only to increase resistance to change. They get into a defensive mode and harden their position. Their defense may take the form of aggressive, violent counter measures.[2]

Establish Rapport

Ostrom raises a valid point. People tend to be defensive when their position is challenged. So what can the crisis counselor do when confronted with a situation where a woman is desiring to abort her child? Rather than attack the person head on, taking a roundabout approach has been demonstrated to be most effective. What this means is that prior to challenging a woman's position, the counselor must first establish rapport and relationship. This is not necessarily a lengthy task, and yet many counselors struggle to find methods to join with the women they desire to help.

Importance of Positive Demeanor

It should be noted that the counselor's demeanor is important as the research has found that people tend to place greater weight on the comments made by those who are perceived as being positive versus those who seem angry or disapproving. Hence, the counselor should strive to maintain a professional demeanor which offers acceptance for the woman even when her stated plan of action is not condoned.

Position of Generosity and Forgiveness

The research has found that adopting a position of generosity and forgiveness leads to greater cooperation. Offering a counselee a glass of water, a Kleenex when they are crying, or a small candy can engender greater cooperation with the counselor and increase the counselee's willingness to entertain what the counselor has to say. People tend to defend their self-image and thus using the woman's own experience to help her evaluate her circumstances will likely be met with less resistance.

Reframing the Pregnancy Experience

By focusing on the positive aspects of the woman, the counselor can facilitate the process in which a woman becomes more open to entertain alternate points of view. Once rapport is established, discussing the positive aspects of continuing the pregnancy and the losses that will be experienced if the child is aborted will have a greater impact. Additionally, focusing on how continuing the pregnancy will save the life of her child and create many future experiences to enrich the woman's life will help her to recognize the certain loss she will experience if she chooses abortion. In like manner, identifying the specific losses a woman will experience by aborting her child will make it harder for her to choose abortion.

Clarifying Uncertainty

It is known that people do not find uncertainty comfortable and thus will often choose a solution that puts them in control. For those women choosing abortion in an attempt to make their life reflect what they desire, taking the time to help the woman recognize that there are far greater uncertainties in abortion than there are in child rearing can persuade a woman to choose to continue her pregnancy. In child rearing there are many phases that occur as standard. A child is born, she is nursed, she begins to walk, she has birthdays, and she begins to talk, and so on until she grows to become an active member of the family and of society. However, with abortion a woman will face the uncertainty of always wondering if she did the right thing, of increased physical health risks, of risking her future mental and emotional health, and of never knowing her child and what her child would become. For those women seeking to decrease uncertainty, the counselor can help them see how abortion creates uncertainty whereas child rearing brings certainty to their situation.

Limit Discussion of Statistics

Sometimes a counselor may be tempted to provide a variety of statistics in an attempt to convince a woman to continue her pregnancy. However, research has demonstrated that "many people lack basic numerical skills that are essential to maintain their health and make informed medical decisions."[3] What this means is that rattling off statistics, although impressive sounding, will do little to help a woman understand that she is responsible for the life of her unborn child and that she is accountable to properly care for herself and her child.

Develop a Clear Plan

A more effective approach is to help a woman develop a clear plan to care for her health and her child. By developing a concrete plan that details the clear action steps that the woman will take to maintain her health during her pregnancy and beyond will not only increase the likelihood that a woman will continue her pregnancy but will increase the likelihood that she will obtain proper prenatal care for her child. Developing a clear plan has also been shown to increase commitment towards the plan. Thus, if a woman is ambivalent about a pregnancy, the more she participates in planning and completing tasks that support the pregnancy, the more committed to the pregnancy she will become.

Personalizing the Child

Commitment also involves personalizing the child. People tend to attach to people more strongly than to objects. By personalizing the child by using terms such as your child, your baby, or your unborn loved one, a woman will develop increased attachment to her child. Discussion about whether she would prefer a boy or a girl, as well as what names the woman has considered all go towards helping the woman undergo the normal attachment process. The counselor should avoid terms that are depersonalizing such as referring to the child as a fetus or using the impersonal pronoun it in conversation. Even if the woman chooses these impersonal terms, it is the counselor's responsibility to respond using appropriate personalizing language. In addition, discussing the child as the woman's child or the woman's baby will make it harder for her to choose to abort the child consistent with the endowment effect.

Intendedness of Pregnancy

Counselors also need to be sensitive to the level of intendedness that the woman expresses. Intendedness of pregnancy seems to be one of the largest risk factors for abortion. Up to half of all unintended pregnancies result in the abortion of the child. Therefore, regardless of whether a woman says she is not going to abort her child, or if she expresses that it was an unintended pregnancy and she did not want a child, the counselor should be prepared to still address the woman as being at high risk for abortion. Alternately, a pregnant woman who has desired a child has a much lower risk of choosing abortion. This factor must be considered when determining the extent to which a woman requires support and follow up counseling.

Properly Framing Questions

How questions are framed to a woman also can be used to persuade a woman to choose life for her child. A woman's answer to, "Are you against abortion?" means very little as it is too general. However, asking a woman, "Are you against abortion for yourself?" is sufficiently specific to assist the counselor in determining what a woman may be contemplating regarding her pregnancy.

Cognitive Reappraisal

For the woman who is focused on how she does not feel equipped to properly parent a child due to a poor prior experience with her own parents, the use of cognitive reappraisal can be useful. Cognitive reappraisal is the process of addressing a woman's fears by examining her past experiences and working to reappraise or rewrite her understanding of the experiences. For instance, if a woman does not want to continue a pregnancy because she fears letting her child down like her mother let her down, the counselor can explain how by having an abortion the woman is acting like her mother. By choosing to be loving and nurturing towards her child, the woman has the opportunity to serve her child in a way that she desired her mother had done as she was growing up. In this way, her prior experience of being let down can be understood within the context of her own life where circumstances do not develop as she would predict or desire. Again, using the woman's own experience to both help her understand her own fears and to move to act in a way that is honoring to her child and herself, is a method that counselors can utilize to positively persuade a woman to choose what is best for herself and her child.

Overcoming Resistance

In conclusion, when working with women who are contemplating abortion it must be understood that they are contemplating the killing of their child because they desire to do what they want, to preserve the life that they desire, not the life they find themselves to be a part of. As such, the counselor can anticipate significant resistance. To successfully overcome this resistance, the counselor must determine how the woman's egocentrism is manifesting and then work with her in a supportive manner. In this way, the counselor moves the woman from a position of selfishness to a position of recognition of her responsibility to both herself and her child. Dr. Stark summarizes this process when she describes how resistance can be overcome in counselees.

> *Before a patient can relinquish a defense that he has clung to in order not to have to confront certain unbearably painful realities, he must come to appreciate (1) the fact that he is defended, (2) his investment in the defense (in other words, how it serves him), and (3) the price he pays for holding on to it. He must come to understand, first, how his defenses protect him against the pain of knowing the truth about his objects and, then, how they ultimately create far more serious problems for him.*[4]

Acknowledge Selfishness

The counselor can utilize this approach by first acknowledging the selfishness displayed by the woman. A counselor might say, "I really understand how you just desire to have your life back the way it was, how you don't want to have your life plan changed."

Address Investment in Position

Then once the woman feels heard, it is possible to move on to the second step. "I know you are feeling desperate and you are willing to do anything to get what you want in your life. I can see how you believe that any decision that helps you to stay on track with your plans is what is best for you, even if it means killing your child."

Appeal to the Conscience

Eventually the counselor reaches the moment of truth, the point at which the conscience can be appealed to. This is the realization that the woman has resisted acknowledging. In this example the counselor might say, "Yet, I see you desiring to do something that will permanently derail you from your life plans. From what you have shared with me, taking the life of a child, your child, was never a part of who you wanted to become."

It is at this point that the counselor must decide based on the woman's response, should the resistance be supported again to build rapport or has the wall of resistance been broken. If it is the former, then the process continues. The counselor may choose to continue to address the various reasons the woman gives for her desired conduct until again confronting the selfishness by appealing to the conscience. However, if the result is the latter, then the counselor can work with the woman to help her rebuild a plan for herself and her child that is consistent with her conscience. At this point the woman has moved from her position of egocentrism to honoring and considering the life of her child.

Conclusion

This book has examined abortion from many angles. Examining the people who have abortions and their personal experiences, as well as reviewing the history of abortion, have demonstrated the significant ramifications that result from the decision to abort a child. While the practice of abortion has been a societal reality for many years, it does not negate the high price that women who have chosen to abort their children have paid in terms of their physical, emotional, and spiritual well-being.

The abortion debate was reviewed and the highlights were examined to provide counselors with the breadth of knowledge necessary for addressing the issues certain to arise in the crisis pregnancy counseling setting. The research on the impact abortion has on people was also reviewed. This research focused on both how people make decisions, and on the consequences for the women who choose to end the lives of their unborn children through abortion.

As the research has been examined, it has become evident that there is no single theory that explains how people make decisions. It was revealed that people tend not to be rational in their approach to decision making, and that as people we are easily influenced by a variety of factors. Hence, the effective counselor will be able to use the research findings to approach the challenge of both supporting and persuading abortion-minded women so that they ultimately choose life for their children. This persuasion generally is not going to occur through rational argumentation. Generally offering support is not sufficient either to persuade women to choose life. No, what must be overcome is the woman's egocentrism, her selfish desire to craft her life in a manner which does not correspond to her current circumstances; to help her to see that killing is not the solution. This persuasion must take place at the foundational level of the conscience, that God given sense of right and wrong.

Despite what we desire, our conscience is ever present. We try to silence our conscience when it conflicts with our desires, yet the presence of conscience is what usually engenders guilt feelings, which are rightly associated with our wrong doing. The mind may be deceived and emotions can be altered, but our conscience remains steadfast. We as people know what right conduct involves. We as human beings know that abortion is wrong. We know this because of our conscience. What must be done to persuade people determined to kill their children is to appeal to the unchanging arbiter of morality, the conscience.

Chapter Eight

A Comprehensive Flowchart Approach

Research Supported Counselor Interventions for Effective Persuasion

Below is a list of items previously discussed that a counselor can utilize to more effectively persuade a counselee to make moral choices. Although no one approach will be successful all the time, these steps should be adopted and practiced by counselors who desire to be as effective as possible. Additionally, the counselor must always remember that it is the conscience, not the rational mind, which serves as the greatest restraint against immoral conduct. Therefore, the conscience becomes the foundational point of intervention, the point towards which the counselor guides the interaction knowing that appealing to the conscience will bring about the greatest likelihood for saving the life of a child whose mother is considering abortion. The effective counselor will:

1. Establish rapport with the counselee.
2. Maintain a positive and calm demeanor when counseling.
3. Be generous toward and forgiving of the counselee (e.g., offer water, a candy, or tissue when the person is crying).
4. Demonstrate acceptance of the counselee not of the immoral action, or the desire for immoral action.

5. Affirm the positive characteristics and strengths of the counselee.

6. Personalize the questions that are asked of the counselee to obtain not what is believed to be the right answer from the counselee, but to obtain information more closely aligned with what the counselee actually believes is proper conduct for herself.

7. Assess the level of intendedness of the pregnancy.

8. Discuss in concrete terms the positives of continuing the pregnancy (e.g., new member of the family, new memories with birthdays, functioning in accord with God's desire to have the child and raise the child to know God).

9. Discuss the specific losses if abortion were chosen (e.g., the loss of sharing life with the child, not getting to see the child grow up, not being able to experience the unique personality and gifts of the child).

10. Not overwhelm the counselee with numerous statistics.

11. Use cognitive reappraisal and reframing to address fears related to a counselee's past experiences that lead to fear or insecurity related to the pregnancy.

12. Develop a concrete plan with the counselee to focus on attaining and implementing the supports necessary for the child (e.g., prenatal care, housing, a time line for preparing the baby's room).

13. Personalize the unborn child (e.g., use terms like "your baby," and discuss the names for the child that have been considered). This may also involve discussing how the baby has his or her own bodily systems which are unique from the mother's (i.e., beating heart and own circulatory system, brain waves, unique finger prints, the ability to feel pain, and the ability to cry – all of this has occurred by eight to ten weeks of development).

14. Appeal to the conscience to persuade a person to do what is moral.

Reasons for Desiring Abortion: Worldview and Ethics Support Abortion

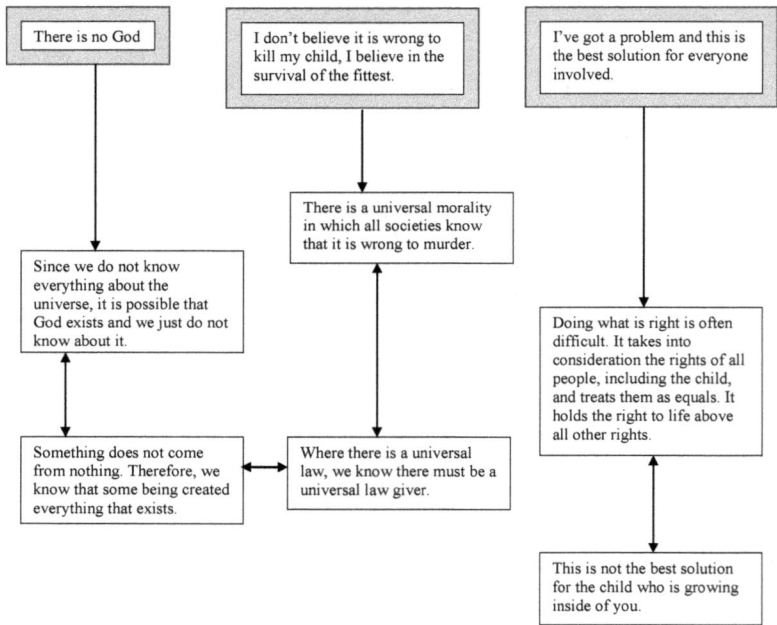

There is no God

I don't believe it is wrong to kill my child, I believe in the survival of the fittest.

I've got a problem and this is the best solution for everyone involved.

There is a universal morality in which all societies know that it is wrong to murder.

Since we do not know everything about the universe, it is possible that God exists and we just do not know about it.

Doing what is right is often difficult. It takes into consideration the rights of all people, including the child, and treats them as equals. It holds the right to life above all other rights.

Something does not come from nothing. Therefore, we know that some being created everything that exists.

Where there is a universal law, we know there must be a universal law giver.

This is not the best solution for the child who is growing inside of you.

Reasons for Abortion: The Unborn Lacks Personhood

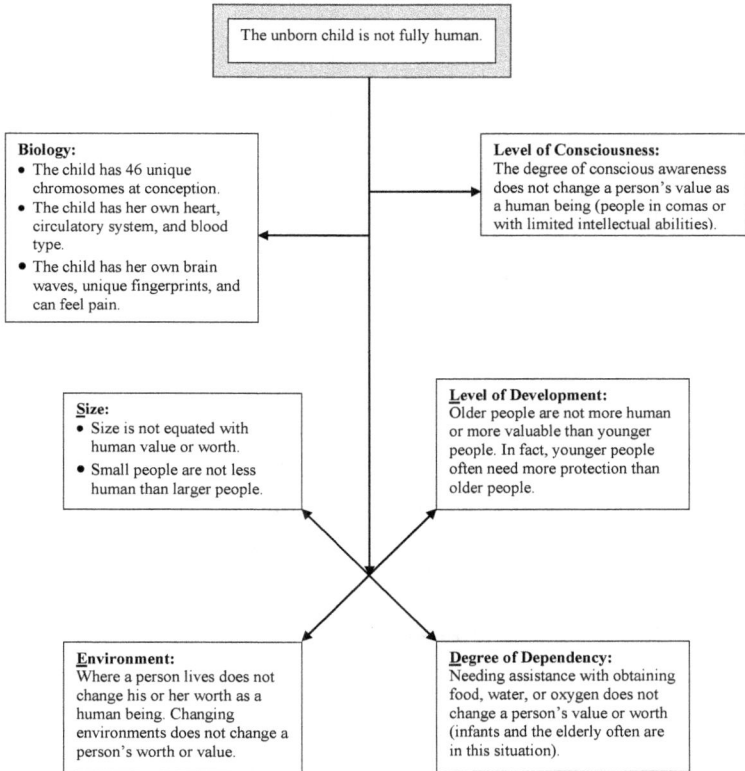

The unborn child is not fully human.

Biology:
- The child has 46 unique chromosomes at conception.
- The child has her own heart, circulatory system, and blood type.
- The child has her own brain waves, unique fingerprints, and can feel pain.

Level of Consciousness:
The degree of conscious awareness does not change a person's value as a human being (people in comas or with limited intellectual abilities).

Size:
- Size is not equated with human value or worth.
- Small people are not less human than larger people.

Level of Development:
Older people are not more human or more valuable than younger people. In fact, younger people often need more protection than older people.

Environment:
Where a person lives does not change his or her worth as a human being. Changing environments does not change a person's worth or value.

Degree of Dependency:
Needing assistance with obtaining food, water, or oxygen does not change a person's value or worth (infants and the elderly often are in this situation).

Reasons for Abortion: Deficiencies in the Unborn

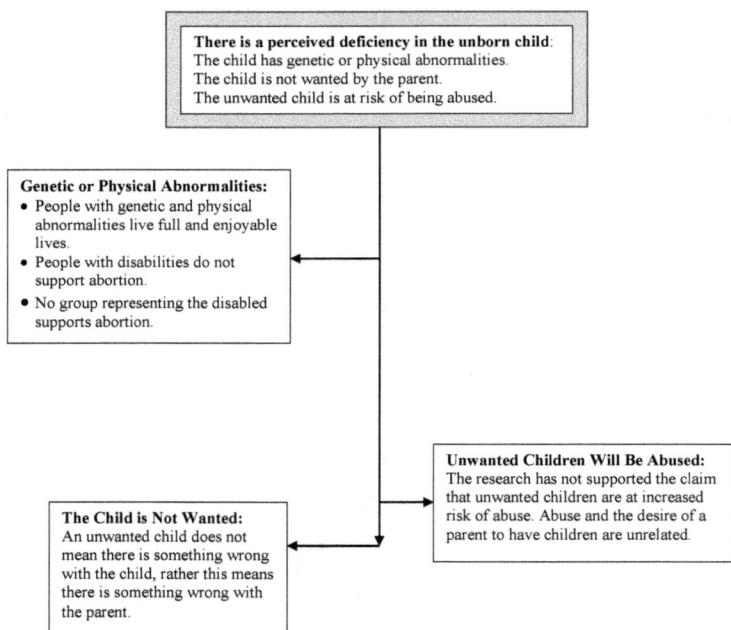

There is a perceived deficiency in the unborn child:
The child has genetic or physical abnormalities.
The child is not wanted by the parent.
The unwanted child is at risk of being abused.

Genetic or Physical Abnormalities:
- People with genetic and physical abnormalities live full and enjoyable lives.
- People with disabilities do not support abortion.
- No group representing the disabled supports abortion.

Unwanted Children Will Be Abused:
The research has not supported the claim that unwanted children are at increased risk of abuse. Abuse and the desire of a parent to have children are unrelated.

The Child is Not Wanted:
An unwanted child does not mean there is something wrong with the child, rather this means there is something wrong with the parent.

Reasons for Abortion: Reasons from the World

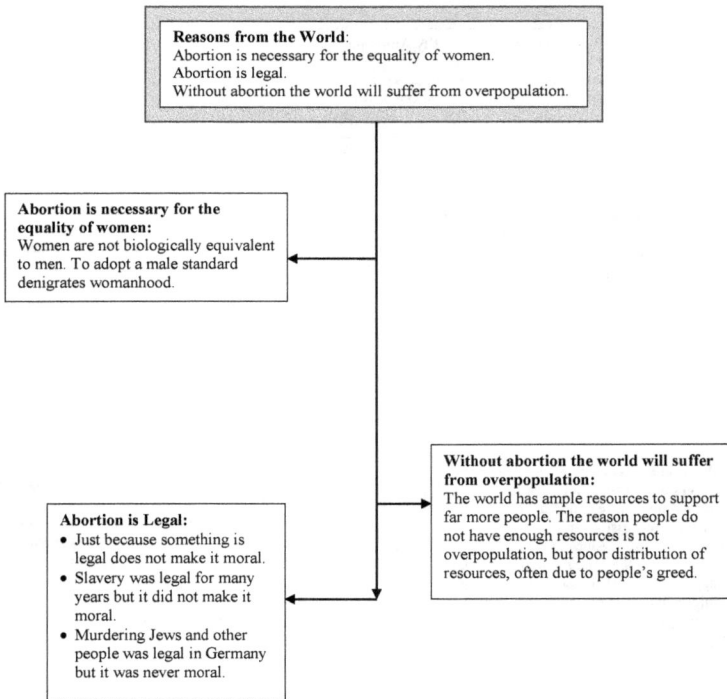

Reasons from the World:
Abortion is necessary for the equality of women.
Abortion is legal.
Without abortion the world will suffer from overpopulation.

Abortion is necessary for the equality of women:
Women are not biologically equivalent to men. To adopt a male standard denigrates womanhood.

Without abortion the world will suffer from overpopulation:
The world has ample resources to support far more people. The reason people do not have enough resources is not overpopulation, but poor distribution of resources, often due to people's greed.

Abortion is Legal:
- Just because something is legal does not make it moral.
- Slavery was legal for many years but it did not make it moral.
- Murdering Jews and other people was legal in Germany but it was never moral.

Reasons for Abortion: Self Based Reasons

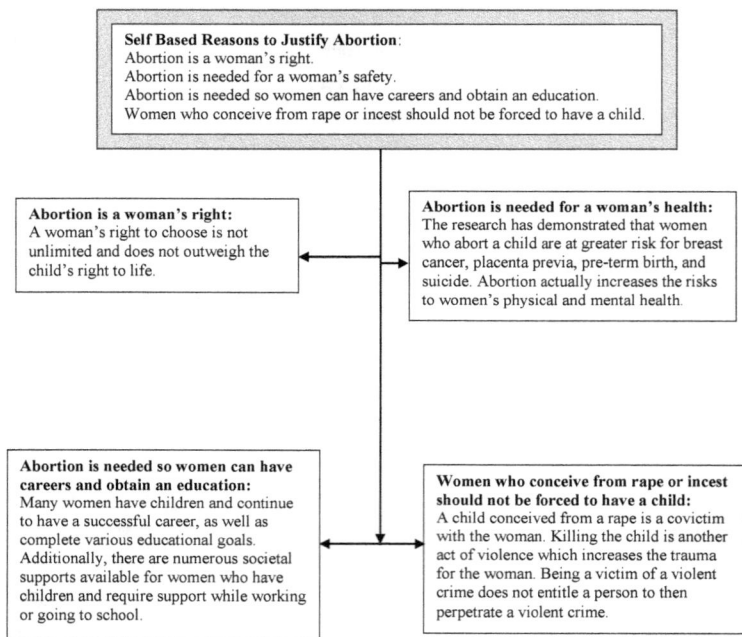

Self Based Reasons to Justify Abortion:
Abortion is a woman's right.
Abortion is needed for a woman's safety.
Abortion is needed so women can have careers and obtain an education.
Women who conceive from rape or incest should not be forced to have a child.

Abortion is a woman's right:
A woman's right to choose is not unlimited and does not outweigh the child's right to life.

Abortion is needed for a woman's health:
The research has demonstrated that women who abort a child are at greater risk for breast cancer, placenta previa, pre-term birth, and suicide. Abortion actually increases the risks to women's physical and mental health.

Abortion is needed so women can have careers and obtain an education:
Many women have children and continue to have a successful career, as well as complete various educational goals. Additionally, there are numerous societal supports available for women who have children and require support while working or going to school.

Women who conceive from rape or incest should not be forced to have a child:
A child conceived from a rape is a covictim with the woman. Killing the child is another act of violence which increases the trauma for the woman. Being a victim of a violent crime does not entitle a person to then perpetrate a violent crime.

Overcoming Resistance

In order for a counselor to overcome an abortion-minded woman's resistance, he or she must address the woman's egocentrism by appealing to her conscience.
1. Acknowledge Selfishness: The counselor acknowledges the woman's self-based reason for desiring an abortion.
2. Address Investment in Position: Address how this position is believed to serve her.
3. Appeal to the Conscience: Identify the price the woman will pay for choosing abortion.

Abortion is a woman's right:
1. I understand how important it is to stand up for your rights.
2. If you do not stand up for your personal rights, who will?
3. If you exercise your rights by having an abortion, you will be taking away your child's right to live. Is this something you really want to live with?

Abortion is needed for a woman's health:
1. I hear how important your health is to you.
2. I understand you feel you will not be able to handle raising a child emotionally and/or physically.
3. If you have an abortion, you are actually placing your health at greater risk and ending the health, the very life of your child.

Abortion is needed so women can have careers and obtain an education:
1. I recognize how important your career / education is to you.
2. I can see how you believe having a child is incompatible with your goals.
3. Is your career / education worth more than your child's life?

Women who conceive from rape or incest should not be forced to have a child:
1. It appears that you feel that having an abortion is the only way to end the suffering you are experiencing from your rape.
2. I recognize that it feels like you are being traumatized over and over when you think about your child who is growing in your womb.
3. Just like you were innocent, your baby is innocent and does not deserve to be harmed or killed.

Appendix

Does Twinning Impact When Life Begins?

It has been argued that defining the beginning of when an individual person begins is complicated by the phenomenon known as monozygotic twinning. An adequate understanding of it is best achieved within the context of the various stages of development that a human child undergoes in his or her earliest days of life.

Initially when the male and female gametes fuse to form a single cell with forty-six chromosomes this new and unique cell is known as the zygote. As the cell begins to divide, it goes through the two, four, and eight cell stages in which the human organism is referred to as an embryo. It is not until later in the development that the name fetus is employed. The primary focus pertinent to twinning involves the first few days of development to perhaps as long as the first two weeks. Beyond the first two weeks after conception, the issue of twinning generally becomes a moot point.

Monozygotic twinning is the process in which a second human child is formed when some of the early cells of the developing child split off and form a separate, although genetically identical, human child. It is still unknown as to whether this process is genetically driven in natural development or if some external force leads to the separation of cells at the earliest stages of development. The twinning phenomena has come to light with the advent of reproductive technological advances in which the fertilization and early division of a human embryo can be accomplished and observed in a laboratory setting apart from the mother's body (i.e., in a petri dish). Of course, observations from artificial environments may not be generalizable to natural environments. Nevertheless, laboratory observations and the associated questions which are generated must still be addressed.

The position that life begins at conception is often charged with being a religiously motivated one. However, as previously demonstrated, non-religious arguments can substantiate that human life begins at conception. It is a scientific fact that the zygote is distinct from the mother and father genetically, making the zygote a truly distinct organism. Secondly, a human zygote, and subsequently the developing human embryo, is genetically human from the very beginning as he or she possesses the genetic material unique to the human species. Lastly, as previously demonstrated, this new zygote is a complete human being, although immature, who will continue by self-directed means to guide his or her development towards greater stages of maturity if afforded the necessary components for all living organisms, namely food, water, and a proper environment. As such, from conception onward, a new human being has come into existence.

Patrick Lee has developed an argument which elucidates this concept in his case for human personhood from conception based in substantial identity. It is as follows:

1. You and I are intrinsically valuable (in the sense that makes us subjects of rights).
2. We are intrinsically valuable because of what we are (what we are essentially).
3. What we are, is each a human, physical organism.
4. Human physical organisms come to be at conception. (A biological proposition: a new and distinct human organism is generated by the fusion of a spermatozoon and an oocyte.)
5. Therefore, what is intrinsically valuable (as a subject of rights) comes to be at conception.

Based on his conclusion, Lee states,

What makes it wrong to kill you or me now would also have been present in the killing of you or me when we existed as adolescents, as toddlers, as infants, but also when we existed as foetuses or embryos.[1]

Despite the scientific biological evidence, there are some who espouse different views claiming that at conception, although a human life may have begun, an individual human person has not come into being given that the potential of twinning exists until approximately the third week of development. Hence, the developing organism cannot be said to be an individual human being requiring protection and a subject of rights until it can be said that the particular human individual is just that, a distinct human individual.

Monozygotic twinning is possible because the cells of the early child, up through the eight cell stage, have the characteristic known as totipotency. This characteristic allows a cell to form into a complete human organism. Totipotent cells exist in an undifferentiated state which is temporary and observed only during the beginning stages of development. As development progresses, the cells of the child differentiate into the various structures and tissue types, and by the end of the second week the cells have effectively differentiated sufficiently that the future course of development has been established. As such, for monozygotic twinning to occur, it must take place in the first two weeks of life.

Recent advances in medical technology have taken advantage of the totipotent nature of early embryonic cells. The use of these cells has allowed for the cloning of organisms to become a reality. In cloning, an adult somatic cell nucleus containing all the genetic material of the mature organism is removed and then transferred into the totipotent embryonic cell of the same organism after removing the nucleus of the totipotent cell. This process is referred to as somatic cell nuclear transfer (SCNT). After the SCNT procedure is performed, the totipotent cell, now with the genetic material of an adult organism, begins to develop and grow as a new organism with identical genetics of the donor.

Cloning has been performed successfully with animals but due to ethical concerns it has not been attempted with human subjects.

However, even in the future event of cloning a human being, it must be noted that the generation of life by combining the complete genetic material from a human being with the ovular cytoplasm of a totipotent cell, if successful, would still be creating an individual human life. Although the method merely simulates the natural process of the male and female gametes coming together to create a full human genetic code and proper cytoplasmic environment, the result is the same: an individual human being who will grow in a self-directed manner towards maturity if afforded the necessary elements to sustain life.

This confronts us with a crucial question: Does the fact that early embryonic cells which possess totipotency indicate that an individual human person has not yet formed? Stated more precisely: Does the potential of monozygotic twinning based in totipotency eliminate the integrity of claiming an individual human being exists during the first two weeks of development?

Let us examine the reasons why monozygotic twinning does not negate the position that human personhood comes into existence at conception. First, "monozygotic twinning is essentially rare, occurring in only three or four out of a thousand births."[2] Although the early embryonic cells apparently have the potential to develop into distinct organisms, it does not appear as if this is the typical developmental course. Rather, scientific observations indicate that the zygote tends to develop into a single individual in nearly every instance.

Thus, having the potential under certain circumstances does not indicate that this is the natural or actual course of a particular cell. In fact, the "test of whether a group of cells constitutes a single organism is whether they form a stable body and function as parts of a whole, self-developing, adaptive unit."[3]

Observations have determined that the cells begin to show differentiation as early as the two cell stage. From the two cell stage onward the cells exhibit intracellular and intercellular differentiation as the unified young child intrinsically directs her cells to form the various structures and tissues necessary to interact with her environment. This makes further development for herself possible. Without intercellular coordination and interdependence, it would be expected that multiple children would develop rather than a single child being the norm. Since this is not the case, it cannot be successfully argued that cellular potential negates the unified whole of the early child is without merit. As Edwin Hui says, "Cellular totipotency and differentiation are thus not necessarily incompatible and to deny the zygote/early embryo the individuality it possesses on this ground is therefore faulty."[4]

Early totipotent cells may be self-governing in isolation but this is not the case when they are part of a larger unified organism. In the latter case, totipotent cells work in concert with each other to develop the necessary structures for the whole organism. This is observed in what is described as twinning and recombination. As observed only in a laboratory setting, an early embryo may separate into two distinct organisms and then recombine and continue to develop as one organism. It is this observation that is used by some to claim that the inception of an individual person does not take place at conception. It is well known, however, that laboratory events may not occur in the natural world. Further, this process merely shows that the totipotent cells are not in and of themselves destined to become distinct individuals. Rather, in typical development, they work together to form one organism. As Hui details,

> *Rather, at most the facts may indicate that for unknown reasons early embryos may passively divide to become twins or combine and become chimeras. It is important to distinguish what an embryo can do actively from what can passively happen to it. ...the recombination of embryos to form a single chimera has been seen only in laboratory conditions. This fact suggests that early embryos possess a certain regulatory capacity and ability to repair themselves in the event that a substantial part of the organism has been removed or damaged.[5]*

Hui concludes that although the developing child has the ability to twin or repair itself if her tissue is damaged, most children develop from a single zygote without the process of twinning or recombination coming into play. Additionally, his conclusion finds support in an example described by Robert George and Christopher Tollefsen.

Consider the parallel case of the division of a flatworm. Parts of a flatworm have the potential to become a whole flatworm when isolated from the present whole of which they are a part. Yet no one would suggest that prior to the division of a flatworm to produce two whole flatworms, the original flatworm was not a unitary individual. Likewise, at the early stages of human embryonic development, before specialization by the cells has progressed very far, the cells or groups of cells can become whole organisms if they are divided and have an appropriate environment after the division. But that fact does not in the least indicate that prior to such an extrinsic division the embryo is other than a unitary, self-integrating, actively developing human organism. It certainly does not show that the embryo is a mere clump of cells.[6]

Patrick Lee and Robert George reiterate how despite the various logical possibilities that may apply to twinning, none negate the reality that an individual person exists from the point of conception forward.

First, as a conceptual matter, the possibility of twinning, of splitting into two individuals, provides no evidence at all against the present existence of an individual prior to the splitting taking place. From the fact that A can split into B and C, it simply does not follow, nor does the fact at all suggest that A was not an individual before the division. Logically speaking, there are three possibilities. A might have been an amalgam or aggregate of A and B. But also A might have ceased to exist and B and C have come to be from the constituents that once went into A (though we do not think this is the most plausible account of what happens in human monozygotic twinning). Or, finally, it is possible that A was an individual and is identical with B or C, that is, that a new individual is generated by the splitting off from the whole of which it once was a part (which we think is the most likely account of what goes on in most cases of human monozygotic twinning). So, the mere fact of the division does nothing to show that prior to the division, A could not have been a determinate, single individual (though itself composed of parts).[7]

Hence, despite the argument from monozygotic twinning, the position that an individual human person comes into existence at conception is both defensible and logically sound. As Norman Geisler frames this issue, "Human life has sanctity whether or not it is yet individuated (cf. Gen. 1:27; 9:6)."[8]

In addition to the scientific and biological evidence for a unique human person beginning at conception, this position is consistent with the biblical record. The Scriptural support for life beginning at conception has already been discussed in prior chapters. However, in the context of monozygotic twinning an additional theological issue needs to be mentioned as it relates to the forming of the human person which, of course, includes a human soul.

Although various views on the creation of the human soul exist, the Traducian view, which posits that the two biological parents are used as the instruments to create both the body and the soul in their offspring, has the strongest scriptural support. The Traducian view acknowledges the parents of a child as the instrumental cause while continuing to view God as the efficient cause of both the body and soul.[9] Since human beings are comprised of a unity of both a material and an immaterial nature, it makes sense that the offspring of human beings would have both aspects, the material and immaterial, passed on by their parents.

Traducianism is also most consistent with the whole of Scripture on God's creative process. Since creation was completed on the sixth day and God has rested from creating since then (Gen. 2:2, Heb. 4:4), the views that require God to create a soul each time a human is conceived or born fail to harmonize with Scripture regarding God's creative work. Even more problematic are the views that hold that God created all human souls at some time in the past, entailing that they are waiting for a body to be created for them. The claim that souls pre-exist is contradicted by biblical teaching, and, therefore, it is deemed to be a serious heretical departure from orthodox Christian doctrine.

Hence, the Traducian view that holds that the parents are used by God to create both the body and soul in children is the most scripturally consistent perspective. In addition, the biblical teaching of the doctrine of original sin, which expresses how every person is born with a sin nature makes sense if the parents, as the instrumental cause, transmit their sinful nature to their offspring. It also comports with the biblical teaching that all mankind was in Adam. However, if the perfect God is creating new souls, then it becomes problematic to explain how a perfect God continues to create imperfect souls. Scripture is emphatic that all people are born with a sin nature, a profound moral and spiritual corruption which infects both body and soul.

Lastly, the Traducian view is most consistent with what is most consistent with the possibility of human cloning. Likewise, monozygotic twinning could be viewed as a form of nonsexual reproduction akin to cloning. Traducianism holds that God is not continuing the creative process described in the opening chapters of Genesis, it entails the view that cloning "produces the same kind of life without a new creation."[10] In contrast to rival views, which find it baffling how distinctively human life could result from cloning, Traducianism has a viable explanation in the fact that the source of the cloned humans is other humans who transmit their nature to them. Other views certainly struggle to explain how a new human life could come from the cloning process.

In conclusion, there are cogent reasons to reject the position that monozygotic twinning precludes the recognition that an individual human person is present from the moment of conception, and, thus, not after the first two weeks of development. The twinning phenomena, therefore, does not create a problem for Christian theology; in fact, it comports with it and it finds definitive support from all of the relevant evidence. The case for the beginning of human life at conception is well-established by the most rigorous analysis and all the pertinent data. Whether an individual human person is formed through sexual means and the typical fusion of gametes or through the splitting or budding that occurs with monozygotic twinning, a distinct and unified individual human person has come into existence. Thus as Norman Geisler states, "Twinning seems to be neither a necessary nor a sufficient condition to reject the full humanness of the zygote."[11]

The evidence all points to the reality that actual protectable human life begins at conception and the issue of when an individual human person begins becomes a secondary matter. Whether twinning occurs or not, from the point of conception forward a human being exists who is intrinsically valuable and the subject who possesses distinctively human rights.

Endnotes

Chapter 1

1   Robert P. George and Christopher Tollefsen, Embryo: *A Defense of Human Life,* 2nd ed. (Princeton, New Jersey: Witherspoon Institute, Inc., 2011), Kindle Locations 473-475.

2   Lennart Nilsson and Lars Hamberger, *A Child is Born* (New York: Bantam Dell, 2004), 65.

3   Francis J. Beckwith, *Defending Life: A Moral and Legal Case Against Abortion Choice* (New York: Cambridge University Press, 2011), 72.

4   E. Joanne Angelo, "The Psychological Aftermath of Three Decades of Abortion," in *The Cost of "Choice,"* ed. Erika Bachiochi (California: Encounter Books, 2004), 92.

5   T. J. Bosgra, *Abortion: The Bible and the Church* (Ontario: Life Cycle Books, 1987), 226-227.

6   Anna Runkle, *In Good Conscience: A Practical, Emotional, and Spiritual Guide to Deciding Whether to Have an Abortion* (Jossey Bass Publishing, 2002), 37-40.

Chapter 2

1   Runkle, 65.

2   Michael J. Gorman, *Abortion & the Early Church: Christian, Jewish & Pagan Attitudes in the Greco-Roman World* (Eugene, Oregon: Wipf and Stock, 1998), 15.

3   Ibid., 15.

4   Ibid.

5   Ibid., 21.

6   Ibid., 22.

7   Ibid., 26.

8   Ibid., 33.

9   *The Didache*, Chapter 2.

10 Gorman, 49.

11 Ibid., 54.

12 Ibid., 55.

13 Ibid., 47.

14 David Lyon, *Christians & Sociology: To the Challenge of Sociology... A Christian Response* (Illinois: InterVarsity Press, 1976), 48.

15 Walter C. Kaiser, *Toward Old Testament Ethics* (Michigan: Zondervan Publishing House, 1991), 166.

16 Ibid., 168.

17 Bosgra, 7.

18 Gorman, 48.

19 Ibid., 63.

20 Ibid., 66.

21 Ibid., 90.

22 Runkle, 65.

23 National Abortion Federation, "History of Abortion," National Abortion Federation, http://ww.prochoice.org/about_abortion/history_abortion.html (accessed October 16, 2013).

24 Runkle, 66.

25 Nancy Felipe Russo and Jean E. Denious, "Why is Abortion Such a Controversial Issue in the United States?," in *The New Civil War*, eds. Linda J. Beckman and S. Marie Harvey (District of Columbia: American Psychological Association, 1999), 44.

26 National Abortion Federation, "History of Abortion."

27 Serrin M. Foster, "The Feminist Case Against Abortion," in *The Cost of "Choice,"* ed. Erika Bachiochi (California: Encounter Books, 2004), 33.

28 Mary Ann Glendon, "From Culture Wars to Building a Culture of Life," in *The Cost of "Choice,"* ed. Erika Bachiochi (California: Encounter Books, 2004) 7.

29 Gene F. Ostrom, *Why Smart People Do Stupid Things:* Rev. ed. (Bloomington, IN: iUniverse, 2008), Kindle Locations 1764-1765.

30 Ibid., Kindle Locations 2538-2541.

31 Candace C. Crandall, "Three Decades of Empty Promises," in *The Cost of "Choice,"* ed. Erika Bachiochi (California: Encounter Books, 2004), 14.

32 Nancy Felipe Russo and Jean E. Denious, "Why is Abortion Such a Controversial Issue in the United States?," in *The New Civil War*, eds. Linda J. Beckman and S. Marie Harvey (District of Columbia: American Psychological Association, 1999), 44.

33 Erika Bachiochi, "Coming of Age in a Culture of Choice," in *The Cost of "Choice,"* ed. Erika Bachiochi (California: Encounter Books, 2004), 23.

34 Eric Schmitt, "For First Time, Nuclear Families Drop Below 25% of Households" *The New York Times*, May 15, 2001.

35 Bachiochi, 24.

36 Ibid., 26.

37 Ibid., 28.

38 Will Ford, *The Truth About Abortion*, DVD, (EX Ministries, 2007).

39 Russo, 30.

40 Ibid., 32.

41 D. Scott Henderson, "Abortion," D. Scott Henderson, http://dshenderson.com//index.php?option =com_content&task=view&id=18&Itemid=49 (accessed October 8 2013).

42 Brian Wilcox, "Federal Abortion Policy and Politics: 1973 to 1996," in *The New*

Civil War, eds. Linda J. Beckman and S. Marie Harvey (District of Columbia: American Psychological Association, 1999), 7.

43 Bosgra, 1.

44 Runkle, 67,

45 Roe v. Wade, 410 US 113, 129 (1973).

46 Ibid., 153.

47 Ibid., 160.

48 Ibid., 162.

49 Ibid., 163.

50 Glendon, 4.

51 Ibid., 5.

52 Miriam Claire, *The Abortion Dilemma: Personal Views on a Public Issue* (New York: Xlibris, 2013), 46.

53 Ibid., 51.

54 Stanley Hauerwas, *A Community of Character: Toward a Constructive Christian Social Ethic* (London: University of Notre Dame Press, 1986), 218.

55 Bosgra, 2.

56 William Marsiglio and Douglas Diekow, "Men and Abortion: The Gender Politics of Pregnancy Resolution," in *The New Civil War*, eds. Linda J. Beckman and S. Marie Harvey (District of Columbia: American Psychological Association, 1999), 270.

57 Beckwith, 32.

58 Ibid., 33.

59 Glendon, 7.

60 Beckwith, 41.

61 Ibid., 40.

62 Gorman, 14.

63 Russo, 25.

64 Linda W. Prine, "In Sickness and Health: Choosing," *Families, Systems & Health* 20, no. 4 (2002): 435.

65 Beckwith, 3.

66 Ibid.

67 Mark M. Hanna, *Crucial Questions in Apologetics* (Grand Rapids: Baker Book House, 1981), 51.

68 Runkle, 147.

69 Lyon, 64.

70 Hauerwas, 214.

71 Claire, 64.

72 James Davison Hunter, *To Change the World* (New York: Oxford University Press, 2010), 92.

73 Ibid., 227.

74 Paige Comstock Cunningham, "The Supreme Court and the Creation of the Two-Dimensional Woman," in *The Cost of "Choice"*, ed. Erika Bachiochi (California: Encounter Books, 2004), 114.

75 Mark M. Hanna, *Biblical Christianity Truth or Delusion?*, (Xulon Press, 2011), Kindle Location 13017.

Chapter 3

1   George and Tollefsen, Kindle Locations 761-763.
2   Ibid., Kindle Locations 107-108.
3   Ibid., Kindle Locations 3175-3177.
4   Ronald Reagan, *Abortion and the Conscience of the Nation* (Tennessee: Thomas Nelson Publishers, 1984), 22.
5   Ibid., 24.
6   Roger L. Shinn "Personal Decisions and Social Policies in a Pluralist Society" in *Abortion: The Moral Issues*, ed. Edward Batchelor, Jr. (New York: Pilgrim Press, 1982), 170.
7   D. Scott Henderson, *Death and Donation: Rethinking Brain Death as a Means from Procuring Transplantable Organs* (Eugene, OR: Wipf and Stock, 2011), Kindle Locations 2504-2507.
8   Norman L. Geisler, *Christian Ethics: Contemporary Issues & Opinions* (Michigan: Baker Academic, 2010), 131.
9   George and Tollefsen, Kindle Locations 1567-1569.
10 Patrick Lee and Robert P. George, *Body-Self Dualism in Contemporary Ethics and Politics* (New York: Cambridge University Press, 2008), 56-57.
11 Ibid., 94.
12 Paul B. Fowler, *Abortion: Toward an Evangelical Consensus* (Oregon: Multnomah Press, 1987), 37.
13 Ibid., 46.
14 Beckwith, 132.
15 Ibid., 159.
16 Ibid., 130.
17 Rushworth M. Kidder, *How Good People Make Tough Choices* (Harper Collins e-books, 2009), 99.
18 Geisler, CE, 157.
19 Ibid., 133.
20 Beckwith, 20.
21 R. C. Sproul, *Abortion: A Rational Look at an Emotional Issue* (Colorado: NavPress, 1990), 129.
22 Geisler, CE, 133.
23 Hauerwas, 199.
24 Bernard N. Nathanson, M.D. and Richard N. Ostling. *Aborting America* (New York: Doubleday & Company, 1979), 188.
25 Ibid., 186.
26 Sproul, 104.
27 George and Tollefsen, Kindle Locations 3019-3022.
28 Ibid., Kindle Locations 1962-1966.
29 Lee and George, 146.
30 Ibid., 149-150.
31 Elizabeth Fox-Genovese, "Abortion: A War on Women" in *The Cost of "Choice,"* ed. Erika Bachiochi (California: Encounter Books, 2004), 58.
32 Bosgra, 20.
33 Ibid., 21.
34 Claire, 178.

35 Elizabeth M. Shadigian, "Reviewing the Evidence, Breaking the Silence: Long-Term Physical and Psychological Health Consequences of Induced Abortion," in *The Cost of "Choice"*, ed. Erika Bachiochi (California: Encounter Books, 2004), 64.

36 Ibid., 69.

37 Nathanson, 193.

38 Geisler, CE, 133.

39 Pricilla K. Coleman, et al., "The Psychology of Abortion: A Review and Suggestions For Future Research," *Psychology and Health* 20, no. 2 (April 2005): 261.

40 Elizabeth Fox-Genovese, "Abortion: A War on Women," in *The Cost of "Choice,"* ed. Erika Bachiochi (California: Encounter Books, 2004), 53.

41 Nancy E. Adler, et al., "Psychological Factors in Abortion: A Review," *American Psychologist* 47, no. 10 (October 1992): 1202.

42 Francis J. Beckwith and Norman L. Geisler, *Matters of Life and Death: Calm Answers to Tough Questions About Abortion and Euthanasia*, (Michigan: Baker Book House, 1991), 82.

43 Sproul, 132.

44 Geisler, CE, 134.

45 Beckwith, 195.

46 George and Tollefsen, Kindle Locations 2562-2563.

47 Fowler, 32.

48 Beckwith, 104.

49 Geisler, CE, 134.

50 Bosgra, 19.

51 Geisler, CE, 164.

52 Fowler, 163.

53 Geisler, CE, 134.

54 Elizabeth R. Schiltz , "Living in the Shadow of Monchberg: Prenatal Testing and Genetic Abortion" in *The Cost of "Choice,"* ed. Erika Bachiochi (California: Encounter Books, 2004), 39-49.

55 Beckwith, 134.

56 Ibid., 111.

57 Ibid., 112.

58 Elizabeth Fox-Genovese, "Abortion: A War on Women," in *The Cost of "Choice,"* ed. Erika Bachiochi (California: Encounter Books, 2004), 59.

59 Fowler, 159.

60 Beckwith, 197.

61 Reagan, 19.

62 Beckwith, 113.

Chapter 4

1 Rushworth M. Kidder, *How Good People Make Tough Choices* (Harper Collins e-books, 2009), 98.

2 Hunter, 6-7.

3 Norman L. Geisler and Frank Turek, *I Don't Have Enough Faith to Be an Atheist,*

(Illinois: Crossway Books, 2004), 22.

4 Geisler, CE, 180.

5 Hauerwas, 215.

6 Hunter, 21-22.

7 Hauerwas, 214.

8 Karen L. Pellegrin and B. Christopher Fruech, "Why Psychologists Don't Think Like Philosophers," *American Psychologist* (November 1994): 970.

9 Pellegrin, 970.

10 Runkle, 2.

11 Claire, 9.

12 Ibid., 28.

13 Ibid., 77.

14 Ibid., 176.

15 Runkle, 4.

16 Lesley Hoggart, "'I'm Pregnant … What Am I Going To Do?': An Examination of Value Judgments and Moral Frameworks in Teenage Pregnancy Decision Making," *Health, Risk & Society* 14, no. 6 (September 2012): 546.

17 Runkle, 4.

18 Sproul, 128.

19 Lyon, 50.

20 Beverly Wildung Harrison "Theology of Pro-choice: A Feminist Perspective," in *Abortion the Moral Issue*, ed. Edward Batchelor Jr. (New York: Pilgrim Press, 1982), 211.

21 Barbara Fisher, Mary Ann Castle, and Joan Mogul Garrity, "A Cognitive Approach to Patient-Centered Abortion Care," in *The New Civil War*, eds. Linda J. Beckman and S. Marie Harvey, (District of Columbia: American Psychological Association, 1999), 302.

22 Lawrence B. Finer, et al., "Reasons U.S. Women Have Abortions: Quantitative and Qualitative Perspectives," *Perspectives on Sexual and Reproductive Health 37*, no. 3 (September 2005): 118.

23 Adler, 1202.

24 George and Tollefsen, Kindle Locations 1421-1426.

25 George and Tollefsen, Kindle Locations 1435-1438, 1267-1268.

26 Kaiser, 11.

27 Ibid., 5.

28 Ibid., 7.

29 George and Tollefsen, Kindle Locations 1559-1562.

Chapter 5

1 Garry Friesen and Robin Maxson, *Decision Making & the Will of God: A Biblical Alternative to the Traditional View* (Oregon: Multnomah Press, 1982), 35.

2 Ibid., 151-152.

3 David Hardman, *Judgment and Decision Making: Psychological Perspectives*, (United Kingdom: British Psychological Society and Blackwell Publishing Ltd., 2009), 11.

4 Bruno B. Averbeck and Brad Duchaine, "Integration of Social and Utilitarian Factors in Decision Making," *Emotion* 9, no. 5 (2009): 599.

5 Ibid., 606.
6 Geoffrey L. Cohen, "Bridging the Partisan Divide: Self-Affirmation Reduces Ideological Closed-Mindedness and Inflexibility in Negotiation," *Journal of Personality and Social Psychology* 93, no. 3 (2007): 416.
7 Hardman, 71.
8 Scott Plous, *The Psychology of Judgment and Decision Making*, (New York: McGraw-Hill, 1993), 71.
9 Dan Ariely, *Predictably Irrational*. Rev. ed. (New York: Harper Collins e-books, 2010), 177-178.
10 Reid Hastie and Robyn M. Dawes, Rational Choice in an Uncertain World: *The Psychology of Judgment and Decision Making*, (California: Sage Publications, Inc., 2010), 271.
11 Richard P. Larrick, "Motivational Factors in Decision Theories: The Role of Self-Protection," *Psychological Bulletin* 113, no. 3 (1993): 444.
12 Kate Sweeny, "Crisis Decision Theory: Decisions in the Face of Negative Events," *Psychological Bulletin* 134, no. 1 (2008): 70.
13 Ibid., 70.
14 Itzhak Gilboa, *Making Better Decisions: Decision Theory in Practice*, (United Kingdom: John Wiley & Sons, 2011), 123.
15 Hastie, 206.
16 Plous, 22.
17 Ibid., 29.
18 Ibid., 30.
19 Sweeny, 71.
20 Plous, 21.
21 Mark D. Rogerson, "Nonrational Processes in Ethical Decision Making," *American Psychologist* 66, no. 7 (October 2011): 616.
22 Cohen, 416.
23 Cohen, 416, 427.
24 Larrick, 447.
25 Ibid., 446.
26 Plous, 61.
27 Ibid., 21.
28 Ariely, 54.
29 Ibid., 2.
30 Friesen, 248.
31 Hastie, 194.
32 Rogerson, 621.
33 Ibid., 618.
34 Ibid., 614.
35 Hastie, 198.
36 Hardman, 89.
37 Hastie, 305.
38 Averbeck, 606.
39 Ariely, 128.
40 Ibid., 127.
41 Ibid., 131.

Chapter 6

1 Coleman et al., 238.
2 Aida Torres and Jacqueline Darroch Forrest, "Why Do Women Have Abortions?" *Family Planning Perspectives* 20, no. 4 (July/August 1988): 169.
3 Myna L. Friedlander, Theodore J. Kaul, and Carolyn A. Stimel, "Abortion: Predicting the Complexity of the Decision-Making Process," *Women & Health* 9, no. 1 (Spring 1984): 44.
4 Coleman et al., 261.
5 Ibid., 261.
6 Ibid., 239.
7 Ibid., 238.
8 Adler, 1196.
9 Rachel K. Jones, Jacqueline E. Darroch, and Stanley K. Henshaw, "Patterns in the Socioeconomic Characteristics of Women Obtaining Abortions in 2000-2001," *Perspectives on Sexual Reproductive Health* 34, no. 5 (Sep. – Oct., 2002): 226.
10 Ibid., 228.
11 Ibid., 232.
12 Torres, 175.
13 Brenda Major et al., "Abortion and Mental Health: Evaluating the Evidence," *American Psychologist* 64, no. 9 (December 2009): 866.
14 Stanley K. Henshaw, "Barriers to Access to Abortion Services," in *The New Civil War*, eds. Linda J. Beckman and S. Marie Harvey, (District of Columbia: American Psychological Association, 1999), 64.
15 Henshaw, 66.
16 Adler, 1196.
17 Ibid., 1196.
18 Warren B. Miller, "An Empirical Study of the Psychological Antecedents and Consequences of Induced Abortion," *Journal of Social Issues* 48, no. 3 (1992): 88.
19 Friedlander, 51.
20 Ibid., 52.
21 Ibid.
22 Coleman et al., 239.
23 Miller, 89.
24 Ibid., 88.
25 Ibid.
26 John Lydon, et al., "Pregnancy Decision Making as a Significant Life Event: A Commitment Approach," *Journal of Personality and Social Psychology* 71, no. 1 (1996): 148.
27 Ibid., 149.
28 D. G. Wilson Clyne, "Reasons for Abortion," *British Medical Journal* 26 (September 1970): 770.
29 Miller, 89.
30 Coleman et al., 259.
31 Torres, 169.
32 Ibid., 171.
33 Ibid., 172.

34 Ibid.
35 Pricilla K. Coleman and Eileen S. Nelson, "The Quality of Abortion Decisions and College Students' Reports of Post-Abortion *Emotion*al Sequelae and Abortion Attitudes," *Journal of Social and Clinical Psychology* 17, no. 4 (1998): 427.
36 Torres, 175.
37 Laurie C. Porter, "How Women 'Make Sense' of an Unwanted Pregnancy: A Case Study of the Abortion/Live Birth Paradox in Surveillance Research," (PhD diss., Regent University, 2010), 126.
38 Ibid., 178.
39 Torres, 175.
40 Finer, 115.
41 Ibid., 113.
42 Ibid.
43 Serrin M. Foster, "The Feminist Case Against Abortion," in *The Cost of "Choice"*, ed. Erika Bachiochi (California: Encounter Books, 2004), 33.
44 Laura Selena Hussey, "Social Policy and Social Services in Women's Pregnancy Decision-Making: Political and Programmatic Implications," (PhD diss., University of Maryland, College Park, 2006), 206.
45 Ibid., 207.
46 Finer, 117.
47 Ibid., 118.
48 Bertina Loutrice Solomon, "The Influence of Family and Significant Others on Women's Decisions to Obtain an Abortion: A Study of a Northwest Louisiana Abortion Clinic," (PhD diss., University of Louisiana at Monroe, 2011), 90.
49 Cunningham, 117.
50 Major, 884.
51 Adler, 202
52 Lydon, 149.
53 Jeanne Parr Lemkau, "Post-Abortion Adjustment of Health Care Professionals in Training," *American Journal of Orthopsychiatry* 61, no. 1 (January 1991): 96.
54 Ibid., 96.
55 Ibid., 99.
56 Lydon, 150.
57 Coleman and Nelson, 438.
58 Coleman et al., 239.
59 Ibid., 248.
60 Dorinda C. Bordlee, "Abortion-Alternative Legislation and the Law of the Gift", in *The Cost of "Choice"*, ed. Erika Bachiochi (California: Encounter Books, 2004), 136.
61 Claire, 16.
62 Clyne, 770.
63 Coleman et al., 243.
64 Adler, 1200.
65 Coleman et al., 240.
66 Adler, 1200.
67 Ibid.
68 Coleman et al., 244.

69 Ibid.
70 Mary Patricia Conklin and Brian P. O'Connor, "Beliefs About the Fetus as a Moderator of Post-Abortion Psychological Well-Being," *Journal of Social and Clinical Psychology* 14, no. 1 (1995): 89.
71 Conklin, 91.
72 Ibid.
73 Adler, 1200.
74 Lesley Hoggart, "'I'm Pregnant ... What Am I Going To Do?': An Examination of Value Judgments and Moral Frameworks in Teenage Pregnancy Decision Making," *Health, Risk & Society* 14, no. 6 (September 2012): 546.
75 Adler, 1202.
76 Ibid., 1203.
77 Ibid., 1201.
78 Lemkau, 100.
79 Anne Nordal Broen, et al., "Reasons For Induced Abortion and Their Relation to Women's *Emotion*al Distress: A Prospective, Two-Year Follow-Up Study," *General Hospital Psychiatry* 27 (2005): 36-43.
80 Ibid.
81 Miller, 90.
82 Elizabeth M. Shadigan, "Reviewing the Evidence, Breaking the Silence: Long-Term Physical and Psychological Health Consequences of Induced Abortion," in *The Cost of "Choice,"* ed. Erika Bachiochi (California: Encounter Books, 2004), 64.
83 Angela Lanfranchi, "The Abortion – Breast Cancer Link" in *The Cost of "Choice,"* ed. Erika Bachiochi (California: Encounter Books, 2004), 73.
84 Adler, 1202.
85 Ibid., 1201.
86 Coleman and Nelson, 426.
87 Porter, 161.
88 Major et al., 885.

Chapter 7

1 Debra Boyer and David Fine, "Sexual Abuse as a Factor in Adolescent Pregnancy and Child Maltreatment," *Family Planning Perspectives* 24, no. 1 (January/February 1992): 11.
2 Ostrom, Kindle Locations 3245-3250.
3 Valerie F. Reyna et al., "How Numeracy Influences Risk Comprehension and Medical Decision Making," *Psychological Bulletin* 135, no. 6 (2009): 943.
4 Martha Stark, *A Primer on Working with Resistance* (Northvale, New Jersey: Jason Aronson, 1994), 128-129.

APPENDIX

1 Patrick Lee, "The Pro-Life Argument from Substantial Identity: A Defence," *Bioethics 18*, no. 3 (2004): 250.
2 Edwin C. Hui, *At the Beginning of Life: Dilemmas in Theological Bioethics* (Downers Grove: InterVarsity, 2002), 69.

3 Patrick Lee and Robert P. George, 127.
4 Edwin C. Hui, 67.
5 Ibid., 70.
6 Robert P. George and Christopher Tollefsen, Kindle Locations 2228-2235.
7 Patrick Lee and Robert P. George, 123.
8 Norman L. Geisler, *Systematic Theology, Volume Three* (Bloomington: Bethany House, 2004), 29.
9 Ibid., 31-34.
10 Ibid., 34.
11 Ibid., 561.

Bibliography

Adler, Nancy E., Henry P. David, Brenda N. Major, Susan H. Roth, Nancy Felipe Russo, and Gail E. Wyatt. "Psychological Factors in Abortion: A Review." *American Psychologist* 47, no. 10 (October 1992): 1194-1204.

Ariely, Dan. *Predictably Irrational*. Rev. ed. New York: Harper Collins e-books, 2010.

Averbeck, Bruno B., and Brad Duchaine. "Integration of Social and Utilitarian Factors in Decision Making." *Emotion* 9, no. 5 (2009): 599-608.

Bachiochi, Erika. The Cost of "Choice": *Women Evaluate the Impact of Abortion*. California: Encounter Books, 2004.

Batchelor, Edward, Jr. ed. *Abortion: The Moral Issues*. New York: Pilgrim Press, 1982.

Beckman, Linda J. and S. Marie Harvey, eds. *The New Civil War: The Psychology, Culture, and Politics of Abortion*. District of Columbia: American Psychological Association, 1999.

Beckwith, Francis J. *Defending Life: A Moral and Legal Case Against Abortion Choice*. New York: Cambridge University Press, 2011.

Beckwith, Francis J. and Norman L. Geisler. *Matters of Life and Death: Calm Answers to Tough Questions About Abortion and Euthanasia*. Michigan: Baker Book House, 1991.

Birnbaum, Michael H. "New Paradoxes of Risky Decision Making." *Psychological Review* 115, no. 2 (2008): 463-501.

Bosgra, T. J. Abortion: *The Bible and the Church*. Ontario: Life Cycle Books, 1987.

Boyer, Debra, and David Fine. "Sexual Abuse as a Factor in Adolescent Pregnancy and Child Maltreatment." *Family Planning Perspectives* 24, no. 1 (January/ February 1992): 4-19.

Broen, Anne Nordal, Torbjorn Moum, Anne Sejersted Bodtker, and Oivind Ekeberg. "Reasons For Induced Abortion and Their Relation to Women's Emotional Distress: A Prospective, Two-Year Follow-Up Study." *General Hospital Psychiatry* 27 (2005): 36-43.

Carter, John D. and Bruce Narramore. *The Integration of Psychology and Theology*. Grand Rapids, Zondervan, 1979.

Claire, Miriam. The Abortion Dilemma: *Personal Views on a Public Issue*. New York: Xlibris Corporation, 2013.

Clyne, D. G. Wilson. "Reasons for Abortion." *British Medical Journal* 26 (September

1970): 769-770.

Cohen, Geoffrey L., David Sherman, Anthony Bastardi, Lillian Hsu, Michelle McGoey, and Lee Ross. "Bridging the Partisan Divide: Self-Affirmation Reduces Ideological Closed-Mindedness and Inflexibility in Negotiation." *Journal of Personality and Social Psychology* 93, no. 3 (2007): 415-430.

Coleman, Pricilla K., David C. Reardon, Thomas Strahan, and Jesse R. Cougle. "The Psychology of Abortion: A Review and Suggestions For Future Research." *Psychology and Health* 20, no. 2 (April 2005): 237-271.

Coleman, Pricilla K. and Eileen S. Nelson. "The Quality of Abortion Decisions and College Students' Reports of Post-Abortion Emotional Sequelae and Abortion Attitudes." *Journal of Social and Clinical Psychology* 17, no. 4 (1998): 425-442.

Conklin, Mary Patricia and Brian P. O'Connor. "Beliefs About the Fetus as a Moderator of Post-Abortion Psychological Well-Being." *Journal of Social and Clinical Psychology* 14, no. 1 (1995): 76-95.

Einhorn, Hillel J. "The Use of Nonlinear, Noncompensatory Models In Decision Making." *Psychological Bulletin* 73, no. 3 (1970): 221-230.

Elliot Institute. "Forced Abortion in America: A Special Report." www.unfairchoice. info: http://www.unfairchoice.info/pdf/FactSheets/ForcedAbortions.pdf (accessed August 15, 2013).

Finer, Lawrence B., Lori F. Frohwirth, Lindsay A Dauphinee, Susheela Singh, and Ann M. Moore. "Reasons U.S. Women Have Abortions: Quantitative and Qualitative Perspectives." *Perspectives on Sexual and Reproductive Health* 37, no. 3 (September 2005): 110-118.

Ford, Will. *The Truth About Abortion*. DVD. EX Ministries, 2007.

Fowler, Paul B. *Abortion: Toward an Evangelical Consensus*. Oregon: Multnomah Press, 1987.

Friedlander, Myna L., Theodore J. Kaul, and Carolyn A. Stimel. "Abortion: Predicting the Complexity of the Decision-Making Process." *Women & Health* 9, no. 1 (Spring 1984): 43-54.

Friesen, Garry and Robin Maxson. *Decision Making & the Will of God: A Biblical Alternative to the Traditional View*. Oregon: Multnomah Press, 1982.

Gardner, R. F. R. Abortion: *The Personal Dilemma*. Michigan: William. B. Eerdmans Publishing Company, 1973.

Geisler, Norman L. *Christian Ethics: Contemporary Issues & Options*. Michigan: Baker Academic, 2010.

Geisler, Norman L. *Systematic Theology, Volume Three*. Bloomington: Bethany House, 2004.

Geisler, Norman L. and Frank Turek. *I Don't Have Enough Faith to Be an Atheist*. Illinois: Crossway Books, 2004.

George, Robert P. and Christopher Tollefsen. *Embryo: A Defense of Human Life*. 2nd ed. Princeton, New Jersey: Witherspoon Institute, Inc., 2011.

Gilboa, Itzhak. *Making Better Decisions: Decision Theory in Practice*. United Kingdom: John Wiley & Sons, 2011.

Gorman, Michael J. *Abortion & the Early Church: Christian, Jewish & Pagan Attitudes in the Greco-Roman World*. Eugene, Oregon: Wipf and Stock, 1998.

Hanna, Mark M. *Biblical Christianity Truth or Delusion? A Refutation of Contemporary Arguments Against the Christian Faith, with Specific Reference to the Recent Book, The Christian Delusion*, Xulon Press, 2011.

Hanna, Mark M. *Crucial Questions in Apologetics*. Grand Rapids, Baker Book House, 1981.

Hardman, David. *Judgment and Decision Making: Psychological Perspectives*. United Kingdom: British Psychological Society and Blackwell Publishing Ltd., 2009.

Harrison, Beverly Wildung. *Our Right to Choose: Toward a New Ethic of Abortion*. Massachusetts: Beacon Press, 1983.

Hastie, Reid and Robyn M. Dawes. *Rational Choice in an Uncertain World: The Psychology of Judgment and Decision Making*. California: Sage Publications, Inc., 2010.

Hauerwas, Stanley. *A Community of Character: Toward a Constructive Christian Social Ethic*. London: University of Notre Dame Press, 1986.

Heilman, Renata M., Liviu G. Crisan, Daniel Houser, Mircea Miclea, and Andrei C. Miu. "Emotional Regulation and Decision Making Under Risk and Uncertainty." *Emotion* 10, no. 2 (2010): 257-265.

Henderson, D. Scott. "Abortion." http://dshenderson.com//index.php?option=com_content &task=view&id=18&Itemid=49 (accessed October 8, 2013).

Henderson, D. Scott. *Death and Donation: Rethinking Brain Death as a Means for Procuring Transplantable Organs*. Eugene, OR: Wipf and Stock, 2011.

Hoggart, Lesley. "'I'm Pregnant ... What Am I Going To Do?': An Examination of Value Judgments and Moral Frameworks in Teenage Pregnancy Decision Making." *Health, Risk & Society* 14, no. 6 (September 2012): 533-549.

Hui, Edwin C. *At the Beginning of Life: Dilemmas in Theological Bioethics*. Downers Grove: InterVarsity, 2002.

Hunter, James Davison. *To Change the World*. New York: Oxford University Press, 2010.

Hussey, Laura Selena. "Social Policy and Social Services in Women's Pregnancy Decision-Making: Political and Programmatic Implications." PhD diss., University of Maryland, College Park, 2006.

Jones, Rachel K., Jacqueline E. Darroch, and Stanley K. Henshaw. "Patterns in the Socioeconomic Characteristics of Women Obtaining Abortions in 2000-2001." *Perspectives on Sexual and Reproductive Health* 34, no. 5 (September/October 2002): 226-235.

Kaiser, Walter C., Jr. *Toward Old Testament Ethics*. Michigan: Zondervan Publishing House, 1991.

Kanfer, Frederick H. and Arnold P. Goldstein. *Helping People Change*. 4th ed. Needham Heights, Massachusetts: Simon & Schuster, 1991.

Kidder, Rushworth M. *How Good People Make Tough Choices*. Harper Collins e-books, 2009.

Klein, Gary. Sources of Power: *How People Make Decisions*. Massachusetts: The MIT Press, 2001.

Koop, C. Everett, M.D. *The Right to Live; The Right to Die*. Illinois: Tyndale House Publishers, Inc., 1976.

Larrick, Richard P. "Motivational Factors in Decision Theories: The Role of Self-Protection." *Psychological Bulletin* 113, no. 3 (1993): 440-450.

Lee, Patrick. "The Pro-Life Argument from Substantial Identity: A Defence." *Bioethics* 18, no. 3 (2004): 249-263.

Lee, Patrick and Robert P. George. *Body-Self Dualism in Contemporary Ethics and Politics.* New York: Cambridge University Press, 2008.

Lemkau, Jeanne Parr, PhD. "Post-Abortion Adjustment of Health Care Professionals in Training." *American Journal of Orthopsychiatry* 61, no. 1 (January 1991): 92-102.

Luscutoff, Sidney A. and Alan C. Elms. "Advice in the Abortion Decision." *Journal of Counseling Psychology* 22, no. 2 (1975): 140-146.

Lydon, John. Christine Dunkel-Schetter, Catherine L. Cohan, and Tamarha Pierce. "Pregnancy Decision Making as a Significant Life Event: A Commitment Approach." *Journal of Personality and Social Psychology* 71, no. 1 (1996): 141-151.

Lyon, David. Christians & Sociology: *To the Challenge of Sociology ... A Christian Response.* Illinois: InterVarsity Press, 1976.

Major, Brenda, Mark Appelbaum, Linda Beckman, Mary Ann Dutton, Nancy Felipe Russo, and Carolyn West. "Abortion and Mental Health: Evaluating the Evidence." *American Psychologist* 64, no. 9 (December 2009): 863-890.

Major, Brenda, Mark Appelbaum, Linda Beckman, Mary Ann Dutton, Nancy Felipe Russo, and Carolyn West. "American Psychological Association Task Force on Mental Health and Abortion." *Report of the Task Force on Mental Health and Abortion* (2008). http://www.apa.org/pi/wpo/mental-health-abortion-report.pdf (accessed September 28, 2013).

Martin, Doug, Amy Martin, Jason Weber, and Trisha Weber. *Considering Adoption: A Biblical Perspective.* Little Rock, Arkansas: FamilyLife, 2005.

Miller, Warren B. "An Empirical Study of the Psychological Antecedents and Consequences of Induced Abortion." *Journal of Social Issues* 48, no. 3 (1992): 67-93.

Mowen, John C. Judgment Calls: *Making Good Decisions in Difficult Situations.* New York: Simon & Schuster, 1993.

Narramore, Clyde M. *The Psychology of Counseling.* Grand Rapids: Zondervan, 1960.

Nathanson, Bernard N., M.D. and Richard N. Ostling. *Aborting America.* New York: Doubleday & Company, 1979.

National Abortion Federation. "History of Abortion." National Abortion Federation. http://www.prochoice.org/about_abortion/history_abortion.html (accessed October 16, 2013).

Nilsson, Lennart and Lars Hamberger. *A Child is Born.* New York: Bantam Dell, 2004.

Ostrom, Gene F. *Why Smart People Do Stupid Things.* Rev. ed. Bloomington, IN: iUniverse, 2008.

Pellegrin, Karen L. and B. Christopher Fruech. "Why Psychologists Don't Think Like Philosophers." *American Psychologist* (November 1994): 970.

Piper, John and Wayne Grudem, eds. *Recovering Biblical Manhood and Womanhood.* Wheaton: Crossway, 2006.

Plous, Scott. *The Psychology of Judgment and Decision Making.* New York: McGraw-Hill, 1993.

Porter, Laurie C. "How Women 'Make Sense' of an Unwanted Pregnancy: A Case Study of the Abortion/Live Birth Paradox in Surveillance Research." PhD diss., Regent University, 2010.

Prine, Linda W., M.D. "In Sickness and Health: Choosing." *Families, Systems & Health* 20, no. 4 (2002): 431-438.

Reagan, Ronald. *Abortion and the Conscience of the Nation.* Tennessee: Thomas Nelson Publishers, 1984.

Reyna, Valerie F., Wendy L. Nelson, Paul K. Han, and Nathan F. Dieckmann. "How Numeracy Influences Risk Comprehension and Medical Decision Making." *Psychological Bulletin* 135, no. 6 (2009): 943-973.

Rogerson, Mark D., Michael C. Gotttlieb, Mitchell M. Handelsman, Samuel Knapp, and Jeffrey Youngren. "Nonrational Processes in Ethical Decision Making." *American Psychologist* 66, no. 7 (October 2011): 614-623.

Runkle, Anna. *In Good Conscience: A Practical, Emotional, and Spiritual Guide to Deciding Whether to Have an Abortion.* Jossey Bass Publishing, 2002.

Scazzero, Peter. *Emotionally Healthy Spirituality.* Nashville: Thomas Nelson, 2006.

Siegel, Eric. *Predictive Analytics.* Hoboken, New Jersey: John Wiley & Sons, 2013.

Silber, Kathleen and Phylis Speedlin. *Dear Birthmother: Thank You For Our Baby.* San Antonio, Texas: Corona, 1983.

Solomon, Bertina Loutrice. "The Influence of Family and Significant Others on Women's Decisions to Obtain an Abortion: A Study of a Northwest Louisiana Abortion Clinic." PhD diss., University of Louisiana at Monroe, 2011.

Sproul, R. C. *Abortion: A Rational Look at an Emotional Issue.* Colorado: NavPress, 1990.

Stark, Martha. *A Primer on Working with Resistance.* Northvale, New Jersey: Jason Aronson, 1994.

Sweeny, Kate. "Crisis Decision Theory: Decisions in the Face of Negative Events." *Psychological Bulletin* 134, no. 1 (2008): 61-76.

Terry, Randall A. *Operation Rescue.* Springdale, Pennsylvania: Whitaker House, 1988.

Torres, Aida and Jacqueline Darroch Forrest. "Why Do Women Have Abortions?" *Family Planning Perspectives* 20, no. 4 (July/August 1988): 169-176.

Walker, Kenneth F. "Sociology and Psychology in the Prediction of Behaviour." *Psychological Review* 48, no. 5 (September 1941): 443-449.

Wennberg, Robert N. *Life in the Balance: Exploring the Abortion Controversy.* Michigan: William B. Eerdmans Publishing Company, 1990.

Whitehead, John W., ed. *Arresting Abortion.* Westchester, Illinois: Crossway, 1985.

About the Author

David Ross is a bivocational minister and healthcare administrator who currently resides in the Pacific Northwest with his wife. He obtained both a Doctor of Psychology in Clinical Psychology and a Master of Divinity in Christian Apologetics from Veritas Evangelical Seminary. Dr. Ross continues to joyfully use the education, experience, and skills that God has given him to serve his community and his local church. Having worked with thousands of patients in clinical practice and numerous couples facing the decision to abort their child, Dr. Ross has invested his life in helping others to make choices that will honor themselves, others, and God.

www.ingramcontent.com/pod-product-compliance
Lightning Source LLC
Chambersburg PA
CBHW071121280326
41935CB00010B/1074